discoveries

EDL
GO
BOOK **EA**

EDL Go Series Book 5

EDITOR
Elizabeth Zayatz

COMPREHENSION QUESTIONS BY
F. X. Duffy, Jr.

DESIGNER
Mary Dee English

ILLUSTRATORS
John A. McKinzie
Scott Nelson

ART DIRECTOR
Ronald J. Wickham

ISBN 1-55855-665-6

9 10 11 EB 00 99

CONTENTS

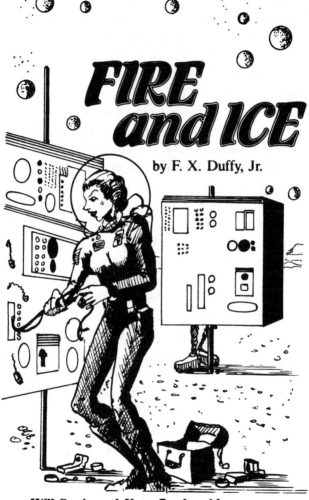

FIRE and ICE

by F. X. Duffy, Jr.

**Will Sonia and Kato fix the old
Earth alarm system in time to save the
frontier planets from the attacking Throps?**

Sonia and Kato had been on the planet Varck for three days. They were trying to fix the old-fashioned alarm device, but had made very little progress.

The alarm system had been manufactured thousands of years ago on Earth. At that time people used a much different kind of electronics. Sonia and Kato were having trouble figuring out how the alarm was supposed to work. But fix it they must, for it was the only alarm system able to withstand the great heat and cold of a Throp attack.

"And why not?" Kato thought. "That is what it was designed to do."

Sonia and Kato had seen dozens of these devices, none of which worked any longer, in the frontier zone. The Earth machinery had been left out in the vacuum of deep space for too long.

Kato's grip slipped and he accidentally let go of the tool in his left hand. He muttered to himself as he saw it float upward, out of his reach. In the zero gravity of the planet Varck, things often floated away.

Sonia heard Kato grumble and looked up. Her face looked very uneasy, worrying Kato even more. Kato knew Sonia had a sixth sense about danger: she always seemed to know something was wrong before it actually happened. Kato looked up, searching Varck's red sky for the savages. He saw nothing, so he calmly asked, "Has anyone ever figured out how these things work?"

"No," Sonia answered, looking very disturbed, "but I think the problem lies in oxygen having been trapped in the device's tiny power cells when it was made." As she talked on, Sonia wished she knew what really was wrong with the alarm system. It was badly needed by the deep-space settlers.

After a thousand-year peace, the savage Throps had started attacking new settlers again. The alarm system on Varck, like other such machinery elsewhere in the frontier zone, would act as an instant messenger. Should the savages cross the time-space line again and attack a planet, the alarm systems would be used to warn the people on other frontier planets.

Only once had Sonia seen the death and ruin that the Throp warriors could bring with them from the other side of time and space. A month ago Sonia and Kato, among others, had been sent to the planet Sidec on a rescue job. The sight there filled them with horror. Sonia would always remember the faces of the dead: screams of pain and terror sealed forever in icy masks.

Sonia forced her thoughts away from this ugly thought and back to fixing the machinery. Its construction was a bit odd, she thought. Then she had an idea.

"Kato," Sonia said into the microphone of her space suit, "maybe we can fix the problem by going to the power source instead of trying to change the electronics of the alarm system."

Kato nodded. He had long since come to trust Sonia's ideas. Their long voyages together had given Kato good reason to believe that Sonia was one of

the best electronics experts in this quarter of the universe. But every now and then, Kato liked to make fun of the fact that Sonia was a human.

Kato started to work on the power source. He raised his hand to remove a part from the alarm. "Um-hmm, that will do it, Sonia! I'll finally be able to fix this heap of metal."

Sonia answered, "Come now, my friend, don't forget earth people are only human and not able to make a perfect machine."

Kato grumbled and made a thumbs down sign with his hand in return. Sonia smiled to herself. She felt better now that Kato could finish the project that had brought them to this gloomy place.

Sonia and Kato made a great team. What's more, their friendship had deepened during their long voyages together. Having faced danger together had also given Sonia a good idea of just how brave Kato could be. Kato truly had great spirit, and Sonia treated Kato with all the dignity and respect he deserved.

4

Suddenly, a high, screeching sound came swooping in from the horizon. A wall of fire hotter than any furnace hit Sonia at the same moment, blinding her with its fierce glow.

"The savages!" Sonia thought. She tried her best to take a step forward toward Kato and the machinery, but hot winds—stronger than a hurricane—threw her back. Heat and wind forced Sonia to bow down lower and lower. Finally, Sonia dug into the blue soil of Varck for safety. She lay helpless in the small, shallow crater of her own

5

making, listening to the sickening sound of a thousand Throp creatures squealing as they attacked.

The temperature around her kept rising. Sonia figured her chances of not burning up were 50-50, mostly because the planet had no atmosphere to trap the heat. If the attack ended soon, Sonia's space suit might keep her alive.

But how was Kato? Sonia tried yelling to her friend, but the awful Throp squeals drowned out her voice. Sonia guessed that if she stayed in her shallow hole, she would probably come out of the attack with her life. But her duty was to save Kato, fix the machinery, and warn other planets that the savages were coming. She breathed in all of the oxygen her lungs could hold from her space suit's backpack and threw herself up, then forward.

Sonia's path took her through layers of glowing white heat. The passing seconds seemed like hours as she struggled blindly toward Kato. Then, to her horror, the temperature dropped suddenly and Varck became colder than ice. The white-hot winds surrounding Sonia had turned into an icy blizzard. Sonia shuddered, drew upon her remaining strength, and moved forward again.

Kato was only a few painful footsteps away. He was leaning against the machinery, his body sagging badly. The closer Sonia got, the more certain she was that Kato had been badly hurt. She tried desperately to move her weary legs faster.

Her legs ached sharply and her breath grew very

shallow. Several times her mind went nearly blank from the struggle and the terrible screeching of the Throps.

Sonia finally reached Kato and found that she'd been right: Kato had blacked out, and his power dials showed that he had little life left. Sonia used the last bit of her strength to bend down and switch on her friend's extra power supply. At the same moment the attack ended.

Sonia awkwardly pushed herself back up to her feet. Then she noticed that Kato's hand was still resting on the machinery's controls. Swiftly, she looked up at the control dials: The alarm system was working again! That's why Kato had stayed with the machinery during the firestorm instead of taking cover. He had fixed the thing and sounded the alarm. The other frontier planets would be ready for the Throp attack. But Kato had paid greatly for his brave deed.

Sadly, Sonia looked down at her nearly dead friend. She put her arms around Kato's sagging body, wanting to comfort him. She prayed that his power cells had not been damaged beyond repair. She bowed her head to his and tried to will Kato's eyes to glow again. Suddenly she heard a crackle.

"Kato?" Sonia whispered with hope.

"Boy, am I ever glad that my mother was a satellite and my father part of an old spaceship," Kato said. "At least *my* parts will always work!"

Kato's aluminum face broke into what Sonia knew was the robot's grin.

Canada to the Rescue

by Margie Hayes Richmond

This is the true story of how the Canadians in Iran rescued six U.S. citizens from Iranian revolutionaries.

There was no advance warning.

November 4, 1979, was a rainy day in Teheran, the capital of Iran. Mark Lijek was working as usual. His second-floor office was only a short distance from the main building of the United States Embassy, where more than fifty Americans worked.

Kim King, a teacher from Oregon, came to the embassy for help and was sent to Lijek's office. King needed a new visa and passport—papers all travelers to other countries must have. He had been in Iran for six months, teaching English to business owners. His visa was out of date and he had lost his passport.

As Lijek and King stood talking, a woman working at the embassy let out a squeal. "They're coming over the wall!" she yelled.

Dozens of Iranian students, some with machine guns, were climbing over the wall that surrounded the embassy. There had been a lot of trouble in Iran since the revolution, and King wondered, "What are those yo-yos doing this time?" Then he heard glass breaking. One of the students was trying to get into the building through a window. A Marine guard knocked him back and fired tear gas. Marine guards also blocked off other windows and doors. Fortunately, many of the windows were protected by a peculiar kind of grillwork which made it

As the Marines tried to radio for help, all their electronic devices went dead. Then the lights went out. The people inside the building sat together in the darkness. They no longer doubted the danger. The Iranians were trying to seize the embassy—and them. They kept their spirits up as best they could—probably by talking about how cheap oil used to be and how to lower income tax levels. One Iranian woman who worked at the embassy even handed out candy.

Gradually they began to talk quietly about the gravity of what was happening. They decided to try to get out. By then Mark Lijek was so indignant about the day's events that he broke the printing plates used for visas.

King and Lijek took a cautious look out the window and saw that the alley next to the building was clear. A Marine forced open a locked back door, and the trapped Americans and Iranians cautiously went out in groups of three. After walking several blocks, the Americans agreed to meet at the British Embassy the next day. Then they split up and went into hiding.

Later that day the news broke: The revolutionary students had captured the American Embassy. The next day, the students attacked the British Embassy.

King was just an ordinary citizen, so it was not too difficult for him to get out of Iran. He got the papers he needed from another embassy, borrowed money for an airline ticket, and flew out of Iran.

The story was different for Americans like Mark

Lijek who worked at the embassy. They knew that the Iranian students had captured more than 50 diplomats at the main building of the American Embassy and were keeping them prisoner. So the Americans who had escaped didn't dare go to their own homes. The Iranians would surely look for them there. They hid as best they could. But the longer they stayed in any one place, the more unsafe they felt.

One of the Americans, Robert Anders, turned to Canada for help. He called someone he knew at the Canadian Embassy. That messenger went directly to Ambassador Kenneth Taylor, the head of the Canadian Embassy in Iran.

On November 10, five U.S. diplomats—Mark and Cora Lijek, Joseph and Kathy Stafford, and Robert Anders—walked up to the Canadian Embassy in bright daylight. They became the "house guests" of the Canadians. On November 22, Henry Lee Schatz, an agricultural agent who had been absent from the U.S. Embassy on the day of the takeover, joined his fellow Americans in hiding. He had been staying with friends since that first day of chaos.

For more than two months, the six Americans hid in the Canadian Embassy. They passed the time by reading and playing card games and Scrabble. They played Scrabble so much that they could figure out what letter was on the front of a square by the grain on its back.

Meanwhile, Ambassador Taylor was working on a plan to get his "guests" out of Iran. Taylor was very worried about what the revolutionary agents might do if they heard about the hideouts. Placing dynamite in the homes or cars of diplomats had become almost a common practice by revolutionaries around the world. Taylor certainly did not want any Canadians or Americans harmed.

Ambassador Taylor began to visit the Iranian Foreign Ministry almost daily. He let the Iranians think he just wanted to keep in touch with his friend, Bruce Laingen. Laingen, among others, was being held prisoner there. Taylor was friendly to the Iranians. He wanted them to think there was no division between Iran and Canada just because the Iranians had taken over the United States Embassy. But what Taylor was really doing during his visits was finding out how the Iranians handled visas and passports.

Next, Ambassador Taylor cut back the number of Canadian diplomats in Iran. They left Iran in small groups at different times. Some took unnecessary flights and used false papers to test and check the planned escape routes for the Americans in hiding. Taylor hoped that all this activity by the Canadians would keep the airport guards from becoming suspicious when the time came for the real escape.

Meanwhile, government leaders in Canada, with the help of United States CIA agents, sent six special passports and false visas to Taylor. The passports had pictures of the Americans with names of Canadians who really would have good reasons for being in Iran.

Everyone tried very hard to keep the hidden Americans a secret. Nevertheless, many news reporters uncovered evidence that some U.S. diplomats had escaped capture and were hiding somewhere in Iran. However, they all agreed not to print the story. But Taylor knew that the secret could accidentally leak out.

A real scare came January 19. Someone called Ambassador Taylor's home and asked for two of the Americans in hiding: Mr. and Mrs. Stafford. Although Mrs. Taylor's heart was beating fast, she calmly told the caller that no one by that name was there. However, the Canadian ambassador and his wife knew then that time was running out.

Ambassador Taylor guessed that the election of new leaders for Iran would create much confusion. So he chose that time to put the escape plan into action. It worked! The six Americans safely boarded a plane and flew out of Iran unnoticed. Later, the four Canadian diplomats still in Iran quietly closed their embassy and left the country too.

When the news of the rescue broke, many Iranians were indignant. One grumbled, "That's illegal!" Another savagely said, "Sooner or later, somewhere in the world, Canada will pay."

The American diplomats spent two days in Germany and then flew to Dover Air Force Base in Delaware. After seeing family members, they met with United States President Jimmy Carter. He called them "six brave Americans." Later, they went to Canada to thank all who had helped with their rescue. Ambassador Taylor was called a smart man with a special dignity, yet full of old-fashioned friendship.

People from all over the United States were thankful to Canada. In Detroit, a huge sign facing towards Canada showed the maple leaf of the Canadian flag and the United States flag side by side. The message was simple: Thank you, Canada!

Ralph gets in trouble no matter how hard he tries to be good.

RALPH

Part 1
When Will You Ever Learn?

by Kay Jordan

The chicken yard was in chaos. Mr. Bud, the prize rooster, staggered around the yard in a most peculiar way. Olive, the best laying hen, squawked, tripped, and banged her head against a fence post. The rest of the chickens were no better as they tried to move about the pen without falling down.

There was no question but that the chickens were drunk. There was no question but that Ralph Garrison was to blame. Of the four Garrison children laughing at the sight, only Ralph would do such a thing. The only question was: When would Ralph ever learn?

Ralph didn't know the answer to that question, although he had an answer for all other questions his parents asked. For example, one day Ralph plowed the furrows in the back field in circles instead of straight lines. Ralph's indignant father did not laugh when Ralph said that Myrtle, the mule, had made that decision. Another time, Ralph strapped wings to his younger sister Rachel and told her that she would be able to fly off the bale of hay. As he'd expected, Rachel dropped right into the fertilizer pen. That time, Ralph's excuse was that he hadn't understood the gravity of the project.

Now Ralph stood again in front of his angry father, who asked: "Why did you harm the chickens?" Ralph answered that he had done no such thing. "Then what," his father asked, "did you do?"

"An act of kindness," Ralph replied.

That answer caused the color to drain from Mr. Garrison's face, a certain sign that an explosion of anger was not far away. "There's not a kernel of truth in that answer, son." Ralph could see that one slip was going to produce a whipping.

"Papa," Ralph said, "when Jim went back to the Navy, he left a bottle. Earlier, I'd asked him wha was in it, and he'd said that the stuff would put hair on my chest. Now, Papa, I have no pressing need for hair on my chest. But those chickens got the molt pretty bad. They're losing feathers right and left. I figured that what would put hair on my chest would do a world of good for feathers. So I gave it to them. I was just trying to help."

"Son, when are you going to learn?" were the last words Ralph heard before the strap came down on his backside.

Later that night the family was kneeling in prayer. Ralph closed his eyes, but instead of praying he thought about what it was that he needed to learn. He began by listing what he already knew.

Ralph knew about agriculture, at least enough to know that he wasn't going to spend his life worrying about drought and harvesting barley. He knew about his family and their way of life, which, if not old-fashioned, was different. He knew the rules of the church, and he knew that he didn't always want to obey those rules. He also knew that he was smart and well liked.

Then what was it Ralph didn't know? Well, he didn't know why jokes came as natural to him as cranberries at Thanksgiving. He didn't know why his parents couldn't enjoy the clouds moving across the horizon or the designs that irrigation made in the soil. "Get back to work," they always yelled. Finally, he didn't know what he wanted to do in life except spend it far away from that tiny area of Oklahoma.

Ralph figured he would probably have to break

the rules of his people to be accepted outside the county. His parents wanted him to accept the rules of the church and stay where he was. He wanted to be someone else, somewhere else. So, Ralph guessed that what his parents wanted him to learn and what he wanted to learn would never be the same.

Ralph was still deep in thought when he heard giggling all around him. Then Papa's voice said, "Ralph, you can stop praying now." Ralph looked up to see his brother and sisters laughing at the fact that he was still kneeling.

George, his older brother, said, "Papa, that's the longest Ralph's been on his knees since the night he fell asleep."

"What were you praying so long for, son?" Papa asked.

Ralph looked up: "The chickens."

Papa shook his head. "Son, when will you ever learn? You don't make fun of prayer. Now, all of you off to bed. Tomorrow's the last day of school, and tomorrow night you have your special program."

Ralph was excited about school ending, but he didn't care about the program because he didn't have a part. The church ran the tiny school, so all plays were taken from the Bible. Even Uncle Mott Adams, the teacher, had to admit that Ralph was the best actor in the school. But Ralph was so naughty that Uncle Mott would cast him only as the Devil, and this year the Devil wasn't needed.

The next afternoon in school, the children worked hard on their roles. From the Garrison family, Grace played the woman at the well and George was the angel who announced that Jesus had risen. While his schoolmates practiced their parts, Ralph winked at Sarah Logan and put horned toads in her lunch pail.

That evening George got sick. Uncle Mott said there was nothing to do but have Ralph take George's part in the play. It was the hottest June night anyone could remember. Ralph didn't look forward to spending the evening dressed up in a sheet to look like an angel, but he agreed.

Ralph stood backstage fanning himself, gasping for air. It taxed him to keep awake. Ralph thought that the only person who had it worse was Henry McDaniel. Henry, who was to play the dead Jesus Christ, was wrapped in layers of cheesecloth. By the time the boys carried Henry off the stage, Ralph was ready to faint.

Uncle Mott pulled one layer of cheesecloth off Henry and put it on the stage floor. He told Ralph to go on and then pulled the curtain. All Ralph could see was a room full of moving fans and water-soaked handkerchiefs. He noticed his Papa loosen his necktie and wipe his neck.

Then the girls came onstage. Ralph said nothing. He had forgotten his lines. Finally the girls asked, "Where is Jesus?" Ralph came alive, furrowed his forehead, looked at the cloth, and answered, "He melted."

Silence fell on the room. Uncle Mott pulled at his hair until it looked like the top of a pineapple. Mr. Garrison was ready to explode. Then laughter started in the back of the room and traveled forward until the entire room was laughing.

After the play, Ralph raced home, claiming that the evening had produced "drought in his body." Actually, Ralph wanted to get away from his sisters, who were talking about his remark, and his parents, who might do more than talk.

When the rest of the Garrisons got home, Ralph was in bed, pretending to be asleep. Mr. Garrison knew better. He stood over Ralph's bed and said, "Well, son, this time you got away with it. Next time, you may not. But son, when are you going to learn?"

Ralph opened one eye and said, "Papa, I wouldn't count on my learning. I think I've played the Devil too many times."

End of Part 1

**Ralph has grown into a young man,
but is no less trouble to his parents than before.**

Part 2
We Sent You Away in Love
by Kay Jordan

The hay bales stood in the field. The machinery was quiet. The harvest was over. Ralph Garrison was tired and lonesome. Harvest time had always meant hard work, but the loneliness was new. With his older brothers and sisters gone, there were no battles with bags of cotton seed at the end of harvest. Only he and Rachel remained, waiting their turns to leave the farm. That was the hard part, the waiting.

Once upon a time, he and Rachel had been close. Now they seldom spoke. Ralph knew he was to blame, just as he was to blame for losing Sarah Logan. Ralph couldn't stand the rules that surrounded his everyday life. So, he spent his free time away from home, drinking and playing cards. His reputation quickly became a threat to both his sister and his first love, Sarah Logan. A vacuum replaced the warmth of close relationships.

Ralph sighed and took out his art pad. He had a lesson with Mrs. Brown that night. They were to decide which of his pictures to enter in the area exhibition for the state art contest. Suddenly, he pictured Rachel leaning over a washtub, her yellow hair blowing in the wind, a look of independence visible on her face. He began to sketch.

Edith Brown had once taught art in a high school, and she'd been giving Ralph private lessons every Thursday night for years. They often laughed at how the lessons began. Ralph and his Pa were in Brown's Paint Store buying plaster when Ralph found a piece of charcoal and started drawing a picture of a coyote-filled prairie on the floor. Ralph was lost on his prairie when he heard Mrs. Brown say, "What a remarkable picture for a young boy. Do you draw a lot?"

"Yep, mostly in my school books," Ralph had answered. "Gets me in a heap of trouble. My best picture was of Adam and Eve. I painted Adam on this foot and Eve on that foot. Teacher tanned my hide. So did Ma. I took it straight from the Bible. Can't help it if God didn't get around to putting no clothes on them."

Mrs. Brown hadn't turned red like Ma when Ralph mentioned no clothes. She had told him to keep the charcoal, along with an art pad, "So you won't have to draw in books." She had also told him to bring her a picture each time he came to town.

A few years later, Mrs. Brown had asked Pa Garrison if she could give Ralph private art lessons on Thursday nights. That was the day the Garrison family came into town to shop. Pa had agreed, and Thursday nights became very special to Ralph. Edith Brown was firm with him. She saw beyond the joking boy to his skill, and she taught him to see beauty.

One day Mr. Brown offered Ralph a job working Sundays, although everyone in town knew the rules of the church people about working on Sundays. Pa Garrison said "No" to the job.

Ralph got mad at the church for attracting attention, at Pa for refusing the job for him, and at Mr. Brown for having offered it. Mrs. Brown had smoothed things over with Pa Garrison, and the art lessons continued.

Overall, Ralph's parents supported his art; they hoped it might help tame their son's wild streak. They even supported Ralph entering the area exhibition, although they questioned his entering the state contest. The contest winners would receive money to attend a state art school, but Ralph's parents were uncomfortable with the reputation of such places.

Ralph talked about the contest at dinner; neither of his parents made any comments about the state contest.

After supper Ralph drove into town. He showed the sketch to Mrs. Brown, and she liked it. Then she said, "I don't want to come between you and your family. I know they want their children to attend church schools. Just remember, whatever happens, there are other ways to become an artist besides going to school."

Those words were hard for Ralph to remember. **He had worked his sketch of Rachel into a painting.**

It won the area exhibition, and Ralph began to have hopes. He never forgot Rachel's surprised and tear-stained face as she saw her picture up on the easel. That evening, his parents talked with Mrs. Brown.

"Ralph will have to win first place in order to go to that school," Pa Garrison said. "Only first-prize money will be enough because Ralph won't get any help from us unless he goes to a college of our faith. Ralph understands how we feel. Anything less will be turned down."

When the state contest came, Ralph, Pa, and Mrs. Brown traveled to Oklahoma City. Ralph sensed the atmosphere of cautious hope in the auditorium. He wished his brother George were alive to share the moment. He was thinking of George when he heard his name called for third place. Full of disappointment, Ralph accepted the bronze award.

That night in the hotel Ralph begged his Pa to let him accept the prize money, but Mr. Garrison refused.

"I'm not standing in the way of your art, son," Pa Garrison said, "only where you learn that art. You earned the award. That's what's important, not the money. You can go to one of our church schools."

"They're not good enough," Ralph objected. "Don't you see that?"

"Good enough for what?" Pa said. "And, yes, I see. I see a country boy who runs after wickedness. You won't be able to say no to the wildness of the city. I won't help you to be worse than what you are."

"But I don't want church school, the church, or anything that goes with it," Ralph said.

"Then you don't want us, your family, and our love," Pa said, "because that's what goes with it."

"No, Pa. I didn't mean that."

"You make the decision on your faith when you no longer live under my roof," Pa said. "Until that time I'll give you all a father can give a child. And that includes my belief in what is true and right."

The next day Mr. Garrison turned down the prize

money offered to Ralph, and the three returned home. Mrs. Brown tried to talk with Ralph about looking into church schools to find the best art program, but Ralph had already made his decision.

The next Thursday, Ralph was absent from his art lesson. When he missed it for the third week in a row, Mrs. Brown sent him a note that read: "Learn to dream as well as you draw." Mrs. Brown didn't try to see Ralph because she knew he blamed her for starting his seemingly hopeless dream.

Ralph ended high school with the worst reputation in the class. The day after school was out, Ralph joined the Navy.

"What about your art?" Pa asked.

"What about it?" Ralph challenged.

The day Ralph left, Rachel and Ma cried all morning. Sarah Logan stopped by and gave Ralph her picture signed, "Your Love."

Pa drove Ralph to the train. They didn't speak on the way. When they passed Brown's Paint Store, Ralph didn't ask to stop. As Ralph was boarding the train, his father grabbed and kissed him.

"Remember, son," Pa said. "We sent you away in love." But Ralph, filled with a deep, raging anger he did not understand, could not answer.

End of Part 2

Ralph Garrison's dream warns him that he must make peace with his father— before it's too late.

RALPH

Part 3
When the Rooster Crowed

by Kay Jordan

The dream was the same: Ralph walked through the ruins of the farm at home looking for signs of life. Nothing was left of the orchard but a lone pear tree. The windmill stood broken and silent against the sky. Hearing only the rustle of the prairie grass, Ralph roamed around the farm. He came upon the two grave plots. The single headstone read: "Ma and Pa Garrison: They never saw the beauty." Ralph knew the motto. The day he left home, Ralph had walked out of the house, looked around, and asked

himself if his parents ever saw the beauty of the land
they worked. A rooster crowed in the dream and
Ralph woke up.

Ralph sat up feeling uneasy, angry, and afraid. He
had come to recognize these feelings as a kind of
hatred of himself, his behavior. He'd had the same
mixture of feelings the day he left for the Navy and
couldn't bring himself to say good-bye to Pa.

Ralph wished the dream would stop. He first had

29

the dream after Rachel had written about Ma's illness. Then yesterday Ralph had received an art magazine. The gift, he knew, was from Mrs. Brown. Ralph felt badly about her too. Maybe that's why he had the dream again. Ralph meant to write Mrs. Brown, but he knew that this letter, just like the letter to Ma, would go unwritten.

Ralph stood up. He had a splitting headache from the previous night's drinking. Paint was on his hands, but he couldn't remember how it got there. Jake and Savage, his two best friends, were not in their beds. Then Jake came in.

"How's your head?" Jake asked.

"I've made a resolution never to touch a drop again," Ralph said.

"Doesn't matter. You'll never be able to live down last night," Jake said.

"What happened?"

"Don't you remember?" Jake went on. "We left Rose's Bar, and you had on a woman's slip. Then you made a pass at a lamppost."

"Did it come home with me?" Ralph asked.

"Naw, the lamppost stayed put," Jake laughed. "Then Savage started playing Chicken Little, yelling 'The sky is falling.' No one paid attention to him, so he climbed the flagpole. When an officer ordered him down, Savage tried to fly. Now he has two plaster casts, one for his broken arm and the other for his broken leg."

Jake eyed his friend. "You don't remember anything, do you, Ralph?"

"No," Ralph answered.

Jake shook his head and said, "You ran off. I later found you in the mess hall. You were painting a tropical picture of the officers in grass skirts. You made the captain the Statue of Liberty, but you forgot his clothes."

"How was the picture?" Ralph asked.

"Pretty bad," Jake answered. "You were painting in the dark. The officers laughed at their pictures, but the captain's going to throw the book at you. But you've got a few days of freedom left. Savage just got a telegram that his dad died, and his mother requested that you return with him. With his broken arm and leg, Savage will need help to get home, and a congressman's son gets requests answered."

"How's Savage?" Ralph asked. "He always said he hated his old man."

"That's what he said, but now he's bawling like a baby," Jake said sadly. "You and Savage don't know when you have it good."

"Me?" Ralph asked, surprised.

"Yeah, you," Jake said. "I never had a family. That's why I don't go to mail call, but someone writes you every day. Anyway, go see Savage, then report to Jones for your orders."

Ralph and Bill Savage left the next afternoon on a two-day train ride to Congressman Savage's home district. Ralph was glad they weren't going to Washington, D.C., where he had visited the Savage family on a previous trip. Ralph had been nervous, especially around Bill's father, even though the man had howled at Ralph's stories.

Mr. Savage had especially liked Ralph's story about voting for his pets in a class election. Ralph had written on the ballot M. Garrison for Myrtle, the mule, and C. Garrison for his dog, Coyote. Congressman Savage had said that with the exception of himself, the Democrats and Republicans had been voting mules and jackasses into public office for years.

When Bill and Ralph arrived at the train station, Congressman Savage's secretary met them. Many people were expected for the memorial service, including the Governor and the Vice-President. Ralph hoped that he wouldn't have to attend. He wished he knew of a way to get out of it without hurting Bill's feelings.

Congressman Savage had represented an agricultural district, and the family home was a large farm. The house was surrounded by cars. Ralph pushed Bill Savage's wheelchair into the house and left Bill with his mother. Ralph looked around before making his way to the kitchen. Shortly afterward, Bill wheeled into the kitchen. He asked Ralph if he would see Mrs. Savage—she was asking for him. Ralph made no comment, but he followed Bill to a room where Mrs. Savage sat on an old-fashioned couch. She motioned for Ralph to sit down and Bill left the room.

"I want to thank you for coming," Mrs. Savage said. "Your friendship means a great deal to Bill, and he will need you. He and his father were a lot alike.

Both were strong-willed. They never got along, but they loved each other. Bill had peculiar ways of showing love, and he thought he needed independence from his father—and his father's success. Anyway, what I really wanted to tell you was that my husband liked you. He spoke several times of your remarkable stories."

"Thank you," Ralph said politely. "And I'm sorry about the Congressman."

"He loved this farm, you know," Mrs. Savage went on. "You're from a farm, aren't you?"

"Yes, ma'am."

"And don't you paint and draw?" Mrs. Savage asked.

"I just scratch around," Ralph said.

"Bill says you sketch beautifully. Your parents are lucky."

"I don't know as they would say that," Ralph said. Then he added, "I don't plan to return to the farm."

"My husband didn't farm," Mrs. Savage said, obviously missing Ralph's point. "He studied law and went to Congress, so he could tell others about the beauty and the hardships of agriculture. Defeat was hard on him. Whenever he would rework a bill, he would say, 'If only they could see what I mean. If only they could see the beauty that could come to the American farm from this bill.' You're lucky that you draw. You don't have to return to the farm to show its beauty to people. Funny how beauty is visible even in the midst of all the hard work and disappointment. Of course, you know that. I bet your parents have your paintings all over their house."

Ralph chose not to comment. Her words had produced an uneasy feeling inside of him—the same feeling that followed his dream. Mrs. Savage continued, and Ralph heard, ". . . so we gave you the east bedroom. You can hear the rooster bright and early."

Ralph remembered the rooster in his dream, and he realized that he was afraid to hear the rooster crow in a house of death. Then he remembered all the unanswered letters, and he knew he couldn't stay. Ralph jumped up.

"Mrs. Savage," Ralph said, "I know this is rude, but would you mind if I went home? If I can get a train out, I can be there in the morning. I'll come back for Bill later in the week."

"Is something wrong?" Mrs. Savage asked, startled.

"Yes, ma'am," Ralph answered. "Something's been wrong for a long time. Bill cried last night when he learned his dad had died. He'd never made up with his dad, and now his dad is gone. My pa's old, and I . . ."

"You needn't explain, son," Mrs. Savage said. "I understand. Just telegraph us when you'll return. And Ralph . . ."

"Yes, ma'am?"

"Say hello to your mule for my husband," Mrs. Savage said. A tear trickled down her face and then she smiled a bit. "My husband said your pet reminded him of a governor he once knew."

The Tower of London is said to be crowded with the ghosts of those who suffered and died there.

The Dread Tower of London

by Arthur Myers

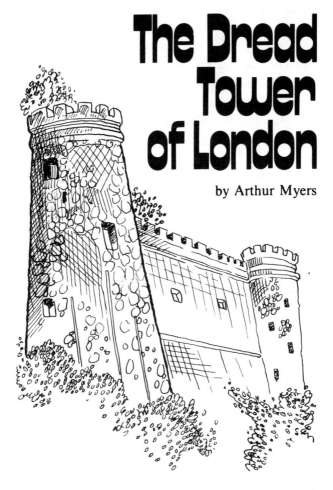

"With her head tucked underneath her arm,
    she walked the Bloody Tower,
"With her head tucked underneath her arm,
    at the midnight hour…"

These lines, along with "Rule, Brittania…" and "God save our gracious king…," must be the most familiar of song openings for millions of Britons.

The lady with the unattached head is Anne Boleyn. She was a wife of King Henry VIII, a man with a habit of ridding himself of wives. She lost her royal head when the king tired of her and ached to marry another lady, Jane Seymour. Katherine Howard, two queens later in Henry VIII's life, also lost her head.

The scene of these dread happenings was the Tower of London. Today, in the opinion of many, the Tower is one of the leading attractions in Britain for vacationers. The Tower may not have the most ghosts to the square foot in the British Isles, but it certainly is said to have a fabulous collection. Queens and dukes, the humble and the grand, suffered and died in its ancient halls. Human spirits, some say, remain where they have experienced strong feelings in life. If true, this would explain the large number of ghosts reported in the Tower.

One evening in 1864, the Captain of the Guard was making his rounds of the Tower. He came upon a member of his company lying motionless on the ground. The soldier's rifle, with bayonet fixed, was flat under him. When the soldier came to, he told a remarkable story: he said he'd seen a white figure come out of the room where Anne Boleyn had spent her last night. The figure glided silently toward him. Startled, he challenged the figure. When it made no reply, he tried to run it through with his bayonet. To his horror, the bayonet went right through the figure. The soldier realized he was seeing the ghost of Anne Boleyn and fell in a dead faint.

At first, the soldier's superiors did not believe him. They thought he had been sleeping, and put him up on charges. But in court, two other soldiers said they had seen the ghost approach the man. Several others said they had also seen the ghost at the same spot, though at different times. The court freed the soldier, and the old legend of the unfortunate queen's ghost was reborn, remaining with the Tower to this day. It certainly has helped the vacation trade.

Not only human spirits roam the Tower, it seems. In the early 1800s, a soldier on guard insisted he was attacked by the horrifying spirit of a huge, vicious, black bear. Where such a monster came from no one seemed to know. The terrified guard stuck to his story and died a few days later, perhaps more or less proving his point.

The Tower of London seems to be tied in with popular songs. Every English schoolchild knows the lines:

"I never know my history,
    the only date that sticks,
Is William the Conqueror,
    and that's 1066..."

And 1066 is also the date when the building of the famous Tower was begun. The man who started its construction was the same William as in the song. He was a Norman duke who stormed across the English Channel and set himself up as King of England, founding what was to become modern Britain. William wanted a strong fort to keep a firm grip on his new capital. Within a hundred years, the project progressed into a castle, with many buildings—including the Tower.

In the course of history, the Tower has been at one time or another a home for royalty, a seat of civil government, a church center, and—for a time—the royal zoo. But today, it is known as a place where miserable pain and savage death awaited people out of favor with those in control of society.

"There is no sadder spot on earth," wrote Thomas Macaulay, a famous English historian, writer, and statesman of the 1800s. Even today, at least in the opinion of those familiar with the Tower's history, an atmosphere of dread hangs in its halls, where the chattering public gathers daily to stare at the old helmets and suits of armor on exhibit.

Names that have been given to parts of the Tower suggest scenes that have taken place there. "Traitors' Gate," for example, is named for the many state prisoners who were brought through it to the Tower. "Little Ease" is a tiny cell where some of them were lodged.

Hundreds of people have died, few from natural causes, in the Tower. Many of them have been famous in their times. One of the earliest prisoners of some reputation to lose his life was Gruffyd of Wales, who broke his neck while trying to escape. Another unfortunate person was Simon of Sudbury, Archbishop of Canterbury. He was dragged from his prayers and beheaded in 1381 by the followers of Wat Tyler, leader of a revolutionary plot against taxes. Then in 1478, George, Duke of Clarence, is said to

have been drowned in a barrel of wine at the Tower.

In modern times, Rudolf Hess, one of Hitler's men, flew to England for some reason of his own and spent a few days in the Tower. Also during World War II, traitors were lined up against a Tower wall and shot.

Death by the ax usually took place on Tower Hill. All told, 75 men, all of high rank, were beheaded there from 1388 to 1747. Lord Lovat is remembered for going to the block roaring with laughter. It seems he enjoyed seeing the viewers' stand break and fall apart, killing a dozen enemies who had come to see him die.

In 1541, a woman was killed by the axman. Her death was unusual in that she did not go quietly, with what was felt to be the proper manners for the event. Magaret, Countess of Salisbury, was the last of the old Plantagenet line and a danger to the Tudors. She was brought to the Tower and kept there for two years. One day in 1541, Henry VIII ordered her death. The order came so suddenly that there was no time to build a stand to hold the block on which to lay her head. The block was laid on the ground, and the old lady—she was then 68—led out.

People about to be beheaded were supposed to carry themselves with dignity and gravity. It was not proper to grumble. They might make a short speech to those in attendance. They might even complain that they were getting a bad rap. But all this was to be done in a most civil manner. They should forgive the headsman and give him a lot of money as a tip for a speedy and painless trip to the next world. One next kneeled, muttered a prayer, and laid one's neck across the block. Then the headsman took over.

But Lady Salisbury wasn't in the mood. She was not guilty, she cried, and would not play the game. The headsman, she shouted, would have to get her as best he could. And she leaped away, to the other side of the block. The headsman chased her, swinging his ax. She was old, and weighed down by skirts. The headsman got her in the end, after a terrible, bloody scene. But many people, to this day, think of Lady Salisbury as one of the great examples of the courage and independence of the Englishwoman.

OIL PATROL

by J. Conaway

**No one suspected what Lucy was up to
—not even her own brother.**

I had flown night patrols over the Gulf of Mexico before, but this time it was different. There were five soldiers in my helicopter. I was piloting a top secret military mission.

The soldiers didn't talk. I wasn't supposed to know why they were going out to Rig 23. They didn't know I had my own private information network—my sister Lucy. She's a drill rig inspector for Petron, a big oil company. She travels a lot, but we manage to talk twice a week by short-wave radio. Our conversation earlier that evening had alarmed me.

"Tomorrow's Mom's birthday," I had reminded her. "You going to be home?"

"Looks like I'll have to miss it," Lucy replied. "We're having some troub...." There was an explosion at the other end of the line.

"Lucy!" I screamed into the microphone.

"YEEEEOW!" she replied. "Don't yell like that."

"Are you all right, Lucy?"

"Just fine," she sang out. "The blasts you're hearing are coming from Rig 23. I'm on Rig 22 now. I wonder what the trouble is. Oops. Someone just handed me my orders. I'm to get over to Rig 23 and check it out. The instruments are showing leakage of oil. Those explosions probably mean there's an oil-slick fire."

Explosions...oil slicks...the sea in flames....It had been happening too often lately. I'd heard rumors of secret agents, bombs, international terrorists. Their plot was to destroy "Big Oil" and so bring the Western nations to their knees. Petron was a likely target for the terrorists. And my kid sister was flying right into the bull's-eye!

"Lucy!" I shrieked in panic.

"Yes, Larry?" she answered calmly.

I suddenly remembered that Lucy didn't take kindly to being treated like a breakable china doll. I found myself stammering, "Er...uh...Lucy, uh, are you sure you ought to be...I mean, well...take care of yourself, Lucy."

I heard Lucy laugh before she signed off. Worried, I walked back to the pilots' room and threw myself down on my bunk. A while later, they called over the loudspeakers for a volunteer to fly five soldiers on a "dangerous mission." I guess I figured that Lucy shouldn't get all the fun, so I signed up.

That shows you how rattled I was. Normally I'm not the hero sort. By the time I'd strapped myself into the helicopter, I was feeling stupid. I told myself that I was a fool not to be back safely playing cards with Sunny Joe. But there was no turning back.

As the soldiers jumped into the helicopter, I sighed for the piles of coins I could be winning from Sunny Joe. Then Major Jenkins climbed in and ordered me to head for Rig 23. I forgot about my usual card game and thought only of Lucy.

We took off in a swirl of fog, which was soon replaced by howling winds. It seemed like hours before we saw the lights of the drilling platform.

"Check your weapons," ordered Major Jenkins. The men obeyed without comment. Five automatic rifles clicked. The men snapped on their helmets and tightened their belts.

I hovered over the landing area for a few seconds, then touched down softly. Figures in orange ran out to tie down the helicopter.

"The colonel has the terrorists trapped down on Level F," one of the deck crew reported to the major.

"OK, men!" growled the major. "This is it!"

A strong ocean wind blasted us as we opened the doors. Bent at the waist, the soldiers dashed for the elevators, gripping their weapons tightly. I dashed after them, but the major grabbed me. He steered me toward a door marked "OPERATIONS." We walked down a short hall and stopped at a door that read "Director—Official Use Only."

"This is where you stay," said the major. "And don't come out until I say so."

I closed the door behind me, not knowing what to think. I moved toward the large glass windows, which were glowing in the first light of dawn. Then I saw I was not alone.

My sister Lucy was in a corner, bent over a large panel of instruments. Her face lit up when she saw me. But I noticed that her face looked drawn and worried.

"Be with you in a minute, Larry. It's almost over," she said and then began barking orders into a microphone on the desk.

I walked over to the windows and looked out. To someone who loves the sea as I do, it was not a pretty sight. Although the oil-slick fire had been put out, the huge black oil slick still stretched out over the water. It was hundreds of yards long, and getting bigger by the minute. The wind was blowing the slick away from us, toward the coast, 53 miles (85 kilometers) away.

We heard Major Jenkins' booming voice in the hall: "All clear below!"

"Jenkins must have captured the terrorists," I said.

"Good show!" Lucy said. "Now we attack that slick!"

Lucy turned back to the control board. The door opened and two engineers came in. One took Lucy's place and the other got busy on the radio.

It was right about then that the truth began to dawn on me. People were taking orders from Lucy!

"There he is!" crowed Lucy. "Big Jim!" A small boat with yellow and red stripes was pulling up to the rig. Those bright stripes were known to everyone along the coast. Big Jim Santos was the best oilman in the business. Petron had hired him to stop the leak. As I watched, four divers plunged off the striped boat into the oily water. They kept diving at regular intervals, trying to locate the leak.

Meanwhile, a fleet had appeared on the horizon. There were about a dozen ships, odd, round ones, bobbing on the waves like apples in a tub. They spread out, trying to surround the slick. The ships' pumps were turned on. The "vacuum-cleaner" process had begun. With luck, much of the oil would be removed on the spot.

Major Jenkins walked into the room. To my amazement, he stepped up to my sister—and saluted! "Mission accomplished, Colonel," he said. Lucy returned the salute and then shook the major's hand. The soldiers came in, dragging their desperate prisoners. More surprises. It was the Alvarez gang—their "WANTED" posters had hung in the pilots' room for years!

Overcome, I sank into a chair. My sister ordered everyone out and rushed to my side. "Are you all right, Larry?" she asked.

I laughed and saluted. "Perfectly—*Colonel*," I said and saluted again. "How long have you been with the government?"

"Ten years," Lucy replied cautiously. "Ever since I joined Petron. The Federal agents had received some hints that the Alvarez gang was operating from within the Petron organization. I was asked to come up with hard evidence. They figured no one would suspect me of being a government agent. I've been really hot on their trail for the last two years."

"Which explains why you've been traveling so much," I finished for her.

Lucy sighed and sank into a chair. She buried her face in her hands. Then she rubbed her eyes and shook her head. I saw how exhausted she was—too tired even to realize her victory.

Suddenly Lucy looked up and smiled. "Hey!" she said. "Let's get in that helicopter of yours and fly back to the coast. We'll be home in plenty of time to take Mom out to dinner!"

Armed with only a microscope and an idea, Robert Koch revolutionized medical science.

The Shy Country Doctor

by F. X. Duffy, Jr.

A little more than a hundred years ago, a shy country doctor walked into the highly regarded Botanical Institute in Breslau, Germany. He brought with him exhibits and a set of findings that would revolutionize medical science. Robert Koch, M.D., upset the scientific world of his day by proving beyond a doubt that anthrax, the most deadly and dreaded disease common among farm animals, was in fact caused by one type of bacteria. This was a first in medical science. It marked the beginning of the modern germ theory of diseases.

Koch's discovery was all the more remarkable because he lacked expensive equipment to work with. Also, he did his experiments without any help or advice from the world's leading scientists. Indeed, Robert Koch was a complete unknown when he first made his findings on anthrax public. Within a year, Koch's discovery was the talk of every medical convention and congress in the world.

Koch's work on anthrax was just the start of a remarkable career. In his lifetime, Koch found or helped directly to find the germs that caused diphtheria, cholera, and tuberculosis. Each is a dreaded, contagious disease that had claimed thousands of lives yearly.

Cholera, diphtheria, and tuberculosis were especially horrible diseases for people in Koch's day. A high fever, stomach pain, and certain death came within hours with cholera. A slow, painful death awaited anyone with diphtheria, which caused a fever and difficulty in breathing. Tuberculosis, or the "white plague," was the most common illness in Europe at that time. One out of every seven deaths was the direct result of this disease, which caused people to slowly waste away. No cure for any of these diseases was possible then, partly because their causes were unknown.

Born in 1843 in the town of Klausthal, Germany, Robert Koch was one of 13 children of a shoemaker. In those days a son followed in his father's footsteps. So, as soon as Robert Koch was old enough, he began his training as a shoemaker. But the family fortunes took an unexpected turn for the better, and Koch was able to start medical studies instead.

In 1862, at the age of nineteen, Koch enrolled at the University of Göttingen as a medical student. Göttingen had the most advanced medical school in all of Europe at that time. Many of Koch's teachers had just returned from Paris with daring new ideas. They not only put these ideas to use in their research on diseases but also had the courage to teach these ideas to their students. It's therefore not surprising that the scientists teaching and studying at the University of Göttingen were making great advances in medicine.

One of Koch's teachers was Dr. Jacob Henle, one of the world's experts on the microscope and a strong supporter of the revolutionary and still unproven theory that living carriers spread diseases.

Young Koch did very well in his studies and won a school prize for his research paper. Upon finishing his studies in 1866, Koch took a job as a doctor at a city hospital and married one of his cousins, Emmy Fraatz.

Koch wanted to move to the United States, but Emmy, a very strong-willed woman, wanted him to start a general practice in a little German town instead. Koch bowed to Emmy's wishes, but he did not do well at first. Then the Franco-Prussian War started and Koch was called upon to serve at the front as a military doctor.

Koch learned a great deal of medicine at the front. Within a few short weeks, he saw many different kinds of wounds. After the war, Koch was hired as a district medical officer and was at long last able to make a good living.

On his 29th birthday, Emmy gave her husband a marvelous gift: a microscope. At once, Koch decided to use it to take pictures of bacteria. He put together a laboratory full of plates, slides, white mice, and his new microscope in a cramped corner of his medical office. There he began to study anthrax.

Koch's choice of that particular disease was based on research already done by French scientists. This research showed that certain bacteria were always in the blood of anthrax-sick animals. Koch's choice was also based on his personal experience: the highly contagious disease drove many of Koch's farmer neighbors frantic whenever it appeared among their livestock. Only a strict quarantine of infected animals stopped the spread of the grim sickness back then. Farm animals had to be killed so they would not spread the disease to others. It was really a kindness

as well, for the animals suffered greatly and almost always died.

Whenever Koch had a spare moment, he labored with the dangerous disease, trying to find the anthrax germ. He was the first to develop ways of using bright dyes to stain the cells smeared on glass slides. The stain made it possible for him to observe, through his microscope, how living germs grew on glass plates filled with special food for the bacteria. Koch saw cells shaped like rods spread across the pure food inside his special airtight slides.

One day, Koch discovered that spores, or seed cells of the bacteria, were also growing on the plates. He suspected that these spores carried anthrax disease. After finishing sketches of the rod-shaped bacteria and its spores, Koch used a needle to shoot the spores into white mice. They all perished from anthrax.

After three painstaking years of study, Koch could say with certainty that the spores triggered anthrax. His patience had paid off, for his experiment proved the germ theory of disease: one particular type of bacteria did indeed produce the anthrax disease. If Koch had been at all hasty in his work, he would never have discovered the deadly spores. And, if he had been at all careless when handling the deadly bacteria, he would have caught anthrax and died. As it was, many leading scientists were slow to regard Koch's work as a success, for his experiment totally upset the scientific ideas of the day. It wasn't until many years later that Koch finally won the credit due him as a scientist.

Nonetheless, Koch gained a reputation as a result of his careful work on anthrax. This made it possible for him to get more money for his research. With the money, he was able to buy a new, high-powered microscope and other equipment.

Within months of his marvelous first discovery, Robert Koch was back in his lab, staining slides of unknown bacteria with dyes and taking pictures of them. Soon after, while keeping up a general practice in medicine, Koch found the germs that caused gangrene, another medical first. At the same time, the world's leading scientists were repeating Koch's work on anthrax and getting the same results. All of them congratulated Koch on his work.

In 1880 Koch was offered a position at the Imperial Health Office in Berlin. He accepted at once. There he was given a laboratory, all the money he needed for new equipment, and two full-time helpers. While there, Koch quickly became one of the world's leading scientists in a new and exciting field: the study of bacteria. He solved the mysteries of scores of dreaded diseases. It is a known fact that his discoveries, along with those of Louis Pasteur and others, paved the way for such medical advances as vaccinations and wonder drugs like penicillin.

A Woman's Place Is in the Home?

by Sylvia P. Bloch

Times are changing and more women are entering the workplace. But how do people feel about it.

There are almost 54 million women working in the United States today. And the most surprising growth in the job market is among women who at one time would never have thought about working outside of the home—women who are married with children. Today, nearly two-thirds of women with children under 18 are working. Many of these mothers were working before they had children.

And in many cases, they returned to their jobs a few weeks or months after giving birth. However, a large number of women are returning to work after a number of years, usually after their youngest child goes off to school.

With prices steadily going up, many families are finding that one paycheck is no longer enough to get by on. Also, many men are finding themselves without a job. Therefore, more and more women across the United States are entering the work force. In many areas these changes are accepted as a matter of course. But there are many people who are used to the more old-fashioned value of the husband working and the wife staying home with the children. These people are hit extra hard by the changes in society.

This can be clearly seen in the lives of the inhabitants of small communities in the Appalachian Mountains area in the eastern part of the United States. In states like Kentucky, Tennessee, and West Virginia, for example, there used to be many jobs in logging and mining. But as the supplies of wood and coal get smaller and the number of jobs done by machinery gets larger, more and more men are losing their jobs.

And their wives, who have kept up the family farms for the tobacco and corn to sell in the market and chickens and vegetables to feed the family, have tough choices to make. They see the distress of their husbands at not being able to find a job. But they also see a grim future if there is no money to keep the family going. So even though their husbands are against it, many women are abandoning the role their mothers and grandmothers had set down before them—that of the homemaker—and entering the job market.

Emmy Owens is one such woman. Her husband, Kenny, used to work in a factory, but it shut down in 1983. After a while he found a part-time job as a house painter, but then he lost that too. When Emmy had to go to the hospital, they had no help with the $2,000 bill. "That's when I decided that I had a choice to make," she said. So she left her kitchen and farm for a job with a regular paycheck. She found a job at a fast-food place. She works a 40-hour week and earns $4.35 an hour. Her boss says that he is happy he hired her because she does a wonderful job. Pleased with herself, Emmy is also going to school part-time. She wants to make something of her life.

But she also has to deal with Kenny, who is not happy with the way things are going. Emmy understands how he feels, but there is no stopping her now. "I love my husband. I need him and he needs me. But he's not happy that I am out there in the world and not at home with him. But there's just no other way. And I'm afraid we're drifting apart."

Sarah Carter's marriage did fall apart when she started working. Her husband worked the whole time they were married, but he never wanted her to leave the home. "He always said I could never clean or cook as well as his mother, so why should I even try to get a job. Who would pay me for anything? But I see now that that was his way of trying to keep me tied to him."

But Sarah, along with many others like her, found a way to feel better about herself. She heard about a free program, and it helped her see that there were things she could do. Sarah met and talked with other women, and they realized their lives had value too.

Then there are the women who look for something more once their children are grown and on their own. In many cases, these women are still young—around 40 years old. Appalachian women usually have more babies in their teen-age years, and therefore the job of raising children is over sooner.

Gail Foster grew up in a small mining town and was the oldest of nine brothers and sisters. She got married when she was 14 and had her first baby at 15. By the time she was 21, she had had all four of her children. Now Gail is 39, with no one at home to look after. "By the time my little ones were in school, I realized that I never really had enough time to be just a child. All those years I spent raising my own brothers and sisters when I was still a child myself. And then I just kept doing what I knew best—raising children."

When Gail was 36, she started a special program at school and got enough training to get a job. Now she not only works, but she is studying to become a nurse. "I see that I never had the chance to grow up," Gail said. "But now I have the chance. There are times that I'm so busy working and studying that I don't have the time to sit down and talk with my husband. It's hard. There were so many years that he was in the role of being like a father to me. Now he doesn't know how to deal with me being a grown-up."

Gail's husband is not alone. It is difficult for many men to see their wives go off to work. They feel abandoned. For these men, everything they were raised to believe in about the roles of men and women is being turned upside down. And when their wives are finding jobs, and they are not, it is not easy to feel good about themselves.

Women are not only joining men in the workplace. In many cases women are taking their place. As the men's jobs disappear, women take the new jobs that men don't want. Many of these jobs are in hospitals and nursing homes, in stores and in fast-food places. The men see these jobs as either paying too little or as "women's work." But they feel angry when their wives take these jobs and they have to depend on their wives' paychecks.

But these women are in their jobs mainly to keep from being poor. They are not looking to buy expensive things. They are struggling to keep up during difficult times. They are scared, but they want things to work out for themselves and their families.

The old saying "A woman's place is in the home" needs to be looked at more carefully. Many people believe that because a woman has the children it is her job to raise them. But the roles of men and women do not have to be carved in stone. It is time to think of a woman's place in the same way as a man's place: "A person's place is where he or she wants it to be."

If you haven't had any luck meeting a ghost on land, try the sea.

GHOSTS ON THE HIGH SEAS

by Arthur Myers

When it comes to ghosts on the salty seas, there are several schools of thought. One holds that spirits haunt many a vessel. Another rather alarming idea is that spirits avoid ships because they cannot cross water. An even more saddening point of view is that there are no such things as ghosts in the first place.

But away with such distressing nonsense! Of course there are ghosts! Any self-respecting salt—as a sailor is sometimes called—can reel off tale after tale of ghosts on ships. Some even tell of ships that themselves became ghosts, along with their captains and crews. Ever hear of the *Flying Dutchman*? Well, pull up a chair...

Captain Fokke was a horrible, horrible man. Some say his name was Vanderdecken and others call him Van der Staaten. Everyone agrees that he was a Dutchman who sailed the seas around 1750 and that his character was a complete disaster. He drank, used bad language, and was even known to drag young women aboard his ship against their will. If anyone objected to his disgraceful behavior, Fokke would loose his terrible temper on them. Sometimes he chopped off their heads. Sometimes he hanged them from the masthead. Captain Fokke ran a grim ship.

One day Captain Fokke was steering his sailing vessel through a storm toward the Cape of Good Hope. He was in top form, howling coarse words and waving his fists at the Maker of All Things—including weather. Fokke's crew was terrified at these attacks on God, but because they were even more terrified of Captain Fokke they kept their terrified mouths shut.

The captain went on and on with his vicious comments. He didn't see the heavenly being hovering over him—not until the angel dropped down on the deck before him.

"Captain Fokke," the angel reportedly said, "you have a dirty mouth."

Captain Fokke, of course, flew into an even greater rage. One thing about the captain—he never had the good sense to know when he was in real trouble. More than once he had come within a hair's breadth of losing his captain's license, but luck had always been with him. Fokke had never learned how to be humble.

"Get off my ship," Fokke yelled at the angel, "or I'll tie you to the anchor and drop you over the side!"

This was a foolish threat to make to an angel. The indignant spirit pronounced a peculiar and severe sentence on captain, ship, and crew.

"I sentence you," the angel cried above the savage wind, "to sail forever through this storm!"

And so a ghost ship was born. Since that day Fokke's ship has been sighted from time to time scurrying through the raging winds toward the Cape of Good Hope, but never getting there. The ship—her real name long forgotten—is called the *Flying Dutchman*. On her unending voyage, the craft often changes color, shape, and size. Sometimes she is a schooner, sometimes a three-masted ship, sometimes a square cargo vessel. But whatever her shape, the ship swoops rudderless through the swirling seas.

At times other ships get close enough for their crews to see white-haired men with long beards desperately working the sails of the *Flying Dutchman* and frantically calling for help. But whenever rescue vessels approach the ghost ship, it vanishes in the storm.

Not all spirits are as rough on sailors as Fokke's angel. In fact, some are a great help. For example, there was the ghost that helped Joshua Slocum.

Joshua Slocum was master of his own bark—as small sailing vessels are sometimes called—when, in 1895, someone gave him a small ruin of a boat as a joke. It had lain on a beach in Massachusetts for some seven years. Slocum decided that he would get the last laugh by fixing up the little boat and sailing it around the world alone. And he did just that. His voyage has gone down in history as an example of excellent seamanship. Although Slocum was a great joker, he was always very serious when he told the following story. He insisted till his dying day that it was true.

Slocum departed on his round-the-world voyage from Massachusetts. After he left his first stop, the Azores, he charted a course for Gibraltar. The first day back at sea, he decided to have a feast. He brought out some cheese and plums that had been given him on the Azore Islands. But Slocum ate too much and came down with such a bad stomachache that he could hardly move. As luck would have it, the weather picked that moment to act up. Although in great pain, Slocum managed to take down his sails. Then he went down into his cabin and passed out. When he came to, the boat was plunging through heavy seas.

Slocum went back on deck and, to his amazement, saw a tall man in odd clothing at the wheel. The man tipped his cap, bowed to Slocum, and smiled.

"I have come to do you no harm," the stranger said. "I am one of Columbus's crew. Four hundred years ago, I piloted the *Pinta* across the Atlantic. Lie quiet, Captain. I will guide your ship tonight."

Slocum was in no state to argue, especially with a

ghost. In fact, he urged the pilot to stay on till the next day.

The ghost nodded, then said in a kindly manner, "You did wrong, Captain, to mix cheese with plums. White cheese is never safe unless you know from where it comes."

And if you don't believe that one, how about this story of the *Great Eastern*?

The *Great Eastern* was the largest ship ever to be built up until its time. It was begun in 1854 and was designed to be the pride of the passenger fleet of Great Britain. But bad luck dogged the *Great Eastern* during her entire life. Her designer suffered a stroke while she was being built and died a week after she was floated. On her first voyage, an explosion killed five crewmen and hurt ten others.

Later her captain and two sailors were drowned while going to shore in a small boat. Many other deaths among the crew, as well as four mutinies, were entered in the ship's log. The *Great Eastern* was so big that she was hard to steer. She managed to sink four ships by accidentally running into them. She hit a huge rock in Long Island Sound, tearing open the ship's bottom. She even badly damaged a wharf in New York by bumping into it.

Was there something strange about this huge vessel? Her crew certainly thought so and, as sailors will, they put the blame on a ghost—in fact, two ghosts.

The story went that while the *Great Eastern* was being built, two workers had been trapped between walls down near the bottom of the ship. Desperately, they had pounded on the ship's iron sides to draw attention, but no one had heard them. There was too much other pounding going on in the regular course of building the vessel. And so they were trapped, dying horrible deaths. To get even, their ghosts stayed on board, bringing bad fortune to the great ship and anyone who sailed her.

In 1899, the ship—one of the great white elephants in sea history—was sold to a scrap dealer and broken up. Some say the bones of the two unfortunate workmen were found. But others say no such thing happened.

As in all ghost stories, you can pay your money and take your pick of what to believe—or not to believe.

STRESS

by F. X. Duffy, Jr.

Too much stress can be dangerous to your health. But there are ways to lessen its effect.

Imagine you're taking a stroll, calmly looking in shop windows. Suddenly, you hear a horrible hiss behind you. Into your mind leaps a picture of a serpent, ready to lunge at you. You turn, heart racing, breath shallow, and body tensed. You see nothing but a truck. You realize that the hiss came from the air brakes of the truck, and not from a

poisonous snake after all. Your mind, frantic just a second ago, sends out an "all clear" signal to every part of your body. You continue your stroll, but you no longer enjoy it. You feel like thrashing your way through the crowd coming down the street toward you, rather than walking calmly.

An hour or so later, you may feel unexplainably drowsy, but you may not be able to relax enough to rest. Small worries about work or a loved one creep into your mind, making you more nervous than usual. You have completely forgotten that grim second when you thought a snake was about to attack, but your body has not. It is still tensed, in part, ready either to "fight or flee."

It is a proven fact that everyone reacts to certain kinds of situations—like emergencies, for example—with some degree of stress. We tense up, our breathing speed increases, and our hearts beat more quickly whenever some kind of peril, real or imagined, faces us. It is natural for our bodies to do this. Many scientists and doctors, however, believe that our bodies' natural reaction to stress often ends up causing us more harm than good in today's world.

Stress, they claim, is becoming a serious health problem, particularly in "modern" countries. If not treated, stress can trigger serious sickness in a victim such as severe headaches, high blood pressure, or deadly heart diseases.

Alcoholism—the need to drink—often results from too much stress. Another result of stress is drug addiction (the feeling that you cannot live without taking a certain drug). Scientists have found that Americans are taking nearly five billion tranquilizers (downers), antidepressants (uppers), or sleeping pills each year either to calm themselves down, pick themselves up, or help themselves sleep.

The distressing rise in the use of alcohol by social drinkers and teen-agers in the last ten years is another warning sign that people are experiencing too much stress. Indeed, experts are alarmed at the upswing in the use of pills and alcohol as means for relaxing. Some are even warning that stress is fast becoming the most serious illness facing modern people.

Studies done to date show that the more problems we deal with in order to get through a day, the higher the levels of stress we feel. Noise, overcrowding, having to prove we're better than someone else, the feeling that we do not control our lives any longer: all these are known to produce more and more stress. Change—such as changing jobs, moving away from family and friends, or even becoming a parent—also leads to higher levels of stress in today's world. Then, too, there are many real challenges to one's self, life-style, and friendships that a person must deal with every day. These challenges also produce stress.

Taken separately, each of these problems is not enough to trigger severe stress. But, taken all together, as the body does naturally, these life problems cause tensions to build and build until the body's nervous system reads the next event as a life-threatening attack. This is usually when problems develop.

The more often the low-keyed dangers appear, the more tension a person's body absorbs, until the "fight or flee" reaction of severe stress takes over. A person can no longer turn off the body's automatic stress responses at this point. Your heart may throb and your lungs grow tighter. Your mind, dizzy for a second, will search around, frantically looking for that horrible something to happen. But nothing happens; there is seldom any real danger pressing in on you. So your mind grows more suspicious of your own body's reactions, which produces only more stress. Your stomach may squirm a little and your mind become slightly dizzy again as you realize all this.

Working while feeling all this becomes harder, much harder—especially if the work is a daily chore and there's no one around to talk to. You also can become drowsy after the body has absorbed all the stress it can take. This is because stress causes your body to burn up many more calories than normal, in a much shorter interval. You may begin to feel stiff, for your body is still on guard long after the actual threatening event has passed. So the next phone call, or someone correcting a mistake you've made—any kind of problem—can trigger yet another severe-stress reaction. Even though the problem is not that serious or life-threatening, you experience severe stress because you've not had a chance yet to relax from your last moment of so-called "peril."

Many people turn to drugs or alcohol when this daily build-up of stress becomes too much to live with. They do so because severe stress itself becomes threatening to a person. And no wonder, since stress makes us want to either hit out at someone or scurry away and hide.

Therefore, it is not uncommon for people to fear that their built-up stress will come roaring out, accidentally, at someone they know or love. This fear can produce more stress, for being angry at someone we are close to is not an easy feeling for most of us to accept. Because home and work are two areas in life where most people's feelings are open to attack, there are few places where we can get rid of stress without feeling uncomfortable. Drugs or alcohol attract people most when such personal problems seem to weigh the heaviest and stress is therefore the greatest.

Here's one secret to dealing successfully with severe stress: Find several healthy outlets for relaxing daily. Regular exercise, going to shows or movies, talking honestly with close friends: all these can do

much to lessen a person's stress level. You should also try to solve small problems, finish an important job rather than putting it off, make a decision (whether big or small), or take any other action that gives you the feeling of being in control of your life.

Stress due to noise or overcrowding is more difficult to deal with these days, since so many of us now live in cities. Taking a walk in a park or playing soft music to block out traffic noise are two ways of relaxing during our private moments.

There will, however, always be times when you will feel tense. It is a fact of modern-day life that few people can avoid stress outright. But there is quite a difference between ordinary tension and severe stress. Although states of severe stress may still also occur, their damage to your life and health will be lessened if you find and use healthy outlets and means of relaxing.

**Adam Frisk makes his own decisions
after a blind friend helps him "see."**

by Karen Papagapitos

"I won't hear of it, Adam!" Jim Frisk told his son
over the phone. "You have only one semester of
college left. How can you think of throwing your
education away?"

77

"Please try to understand," Adam said. "I finally know what I want to do. I guess I always knew, but was never able to make the decision on my own. You're the one who wanted me to get a college education. That's all I ever remember you telling me, even when I was in kindergarten."

"Son, I've worked hard all my life to send you to college. Please don't spoil everything now."

"This is my decision, not yours," Adam told his father. "I can't turn back just to please you."

"This will kill your mother, you know that!"

"It's my life!" Adam shouted and slammed down the phone. Lately every call to his father ended in a fight. Why couldn't his dad understand?

"It's no use," Adam thought. "He'll never understand because he doesn't want to." Suddenly Adam felt the need for fresh air.

He walked outside and started toward the student center. He walked through the swinging doors and saw Lisa. She waved him over to her table.

"Hi, Adam," Lisa said. "Sit down and meet my friend Connie."

"Hi, Connie," Adam said as he sat down.

"Connie and I were just talking about the offer you got to study stage acting in New York. Are you going to accept?"

"I don't know," Adam said, thinking about the 25 years his father had put in as a construction worker to send him to college.

"You have a great voice for the stage," Connie said.

"Yeah, thanks," Adam answered. Then he took a good look at Connie. She was looking both at and past him at the same time.

"I'm sorry," Adam said in a hoarse voice. "I didn't realize that you're blind."

"Why are you sorry?" Connie asked, a smile playing at the corners of her mouth. "It's not your fault. I don't think twice about it."

"Connie's an artist too," Lisa interrupted. "She draws."

"I don't understand," Adam said.

"Of course not," Connie laughed. "Most people think blind people are naturally clumsy and can learn only simple crafts. I'm working on my master's degree in education, with a specialty in art for the blind. How about letting me sketch you right now?"

"Okay, but get my strong jawline right. It's my best feature," Adam joked.

Connie smiled politely. She touched Adam's face until the memory of every feature was in her fingers. Then she put it on the paper.

"Hey, that's really good!" Adam said as he looked at the finished drawing. "You even got my crooked nose right."

"I call my drawings outlines," Connie answered. "That's because I can't fill them in with color. I've already sold some of them," she added.

"You must be very proud of yourself," Adam said.

"Yes, I feel good about myself," Connie answered. "I set a goal for myself and worked at it, though sometimes it seemed impossible. But I knew if I didn't try—I mean really try—I would be questioning myself all my life. The outline of my life would be unfinished."

"What kept you going?" Adam asked.

"I just kept believing in myself and my instincts."

"I guess your family helped you too," Adam said, a note of jealousy creeping into his voice.

"Are you kidding?" Connie laughed. "Just the opposite. They wanted me to stay home, learn a simple trade, and forget about my art degree. We had some great fights over that."

On the way back to his room, Adam thought about Connie. He loved acting very much. It gave meaning to his life, helped him relax, and even helped him get through tough exams. The question bothering Adam now was why he had stayed in college all these years. Was it just because his father had wanted him to? Or did he, too, want that college education?

Back in his room, Adam felt drowsy. He lay down on his bed and stared at the markings on the ceiling. Lines ran everywhere, and looking at them made Adam feel dizzy. He closed his eyes for a minute's rest.

Adam was in a swamp. A dense fog surrounded him. Everywhere he sensed peril. He saw serpents squirming on the ground and heard their hiss. Other wild animals were thrashing in a nearby thicket. Adam stood frozen in fear. If he moved, a poisonous snake might strike him, or an immense monster might lunge out of nowhere.

The swamp was full of moving shapes and outlines. Adam couldn't tell whether they were trees or animals because the fog was growing thicker. He was getting frantic now.

Then Adam heard a man's voice: "Over here, Adam. The way's clear here." Adam recognized the voice as his father's.

For some unknown reason, Adam didn't answer his father. He turned in the direction of another voice coming through the fog. It was his own.

"Trust yourself. Find your own way out," the voice said.

Fog, shadows, and outlines started to close in on Adam. Desperately, he grabbed at one of the outlines, not caring whether it was snake or tree. He needed time to think—to find a way out. The two voices were trying to drown each other out.

Adam awoke suddenly. He had only one thought. He had to talk to his father. A telegram would reach him quickly, Adam thought. By phone he sent his message:

DAD
NEED TO TALK ABOUT SITUATION.
SORRY ABOUT BEHAVIOR ON PHONE.
PLEASE COME ON NEXT PLANE.

LOVE
ADAM

Adam's father arrived the next day.

"Hi, son." Mr. Frisk's deep voice reminded Adam of his dream. Walking around the university, Adam and his father talked calmly for the first time in months.

"I've spent a lot of time thinking about my decision to quit school," Adam said. "And I know it's right for me."

"You're not being practical," Adam's father said, shaking his head.

"I can understand why you feel that way, Dad. You quit college 25 years ago to raise a family and you've regretted it ever since. Right?"

"Sure, I often think about never having finished my degree," Adam's father admitted.

"Don't you see, Dad? You're trying to finish your degree through me. And that's not fair."

"I never meant to do that, son," Mr. Frisk said, although he was somewhat doubtful about the truth of his son's statement.

"Listen, why don't you go back to college? There's nothing to stop you now," Adam challenged.

"Sure, sure, I'll think about it," Mr. Frisk answered quickly. "Now, what are you going to do?"

"I need time off from school to see things more clearly," Adam answered. "In the meantime, I'll go to New York to study acting. I don't know whether my final decision will be to finish college or not. I might decide next fall—or maybe in 25 years. But whatever I choose to do, it will be my decision."

"Fair enough," his father said, grateful that his son was still willing to consider the value of an education. He stopped himself from pushing his viewpoint on Adam again. Instead he asked, "Now where can we get some sandwiches and coffee? I'm starving!"

"At the student center," Adam answered.

The two men walked side by side, each lost in thought about the unfinished outline of his own life.

The Secrets of Love

by F. X. Duffy, Jr.

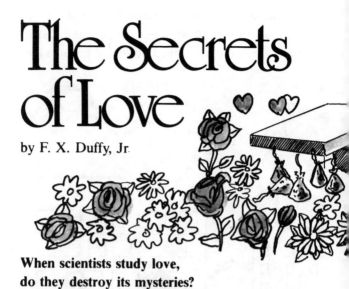

**When scientists study love,
do they destroy its mysteries?**

The scientists began the love experiment in a most unlikely place: at the ends of two bridges running across the mighty Capilano River in British Columbia, Canada. The bridges themselves could not have been more different. One was a well-built, modern bridge. The other was nothing more than a crude, narrow footpath 230 feet (70 meters) above the river.

The scientists wanted to prove that love has much in common with other feelings, such as fear. So on different days, they had a beautiful woman stop men coming off both bridges. She asked the men to fill out a form, which was really just an excuse for her to give them her telephone number.

The results of this curious experiment were interesting to the growing number of scientists studying the tropic highs and arctic lows of romantic love. Few of the men who had calmly walked across the modern bridge called the woman for a date. Most of the calls came from the men who had crossed the dizzying footpath, their hearts throbbing and hands shaking from fear.

Some scientists have gone so far as to suggest that love, like any other feeling, is only the result of a chemical or two floating around in an overworked body. Although this is only a theory, many people are upset by such scientific explanations of love, a region over which poetry used to rule. Senator William Proxmire of Wisconsin is one of these people. He believes that love is not a proper subject for science. But he also admits that he doesn't want an answer to love's mysteries.

Science has yet to find an explanation for love. But in the course of trying, scientists have come up with some interesting facts. For example, more young people today than ever before are attracted by the abandon and distress of romantic love. Further, more than half of the college students questioned in one study said that they would leave their mates if love ever went out of their marriages.

For those of you searching for a true love, experts have a few words of warning. Wondrous joy is only one part of romantic love. In fact, falling in love feels much like being on a dangerous expedition. New lovers experience the same degree of worry as people who have just lost their jobs. And then, of course, there's the aching pain of failure and regret during those dreary days after a breakup.

You may have heard the saying that "opposites attract." "Not so," say love experts. Most people want someone like themselves to love. For example, one researcher gave students at the University of Minnesota the chance to use a computer as a dating service. Most of the students chose dates who matched their own characters, interests, and physical looks.

And then there are the "love junkies." Answer the following questions to see if you are likely to become one.

1. Must you *always* be in a love relationship?

2. Do you always choose to love someone who cannot or will not return your love in full?
3. Do you feel a desperate need for chocolates when a romance breaks up?

If you answered "Yes" to all three questions, you may be on your way to becoming a love junkie. Love junkies are people who *must* be in love. If they're not, they have a difficult time in all other areas of their life.

Scientists have studied the behavior of such people, trying to find some way to prevent them from becoming victims of love. Dr. Donald F. Klein and Dr. Michael R. Liebowitz are two such scientists at the New York State Psychiatric Institute. They believe that romantic love is triggered by the brain's release of a certain chemical. This chemical is very much like the drug commonly known as "speed." And if what Drs. Klein and Liebowitz say is true, people really do get "high" on love. "And the crash that follows breakup is much like drug withdrawal," they say.

While studying the body chemistry of love junkies, Drs. Klein and Liebowitz noted that the lovesick people experienced no relief from mood elevators used to treat great sadness.

Then they made an interesting discovery: almost every one of their heartbroken subjects went through a chocolate-eating stage after breaking up with their love. Chocolate is rich in the same chemical that the brain produces when one falls in love. This drug might someday cure lovesickness much the same way that a bottle of medicine can cure a cough.

In another experiment done at the Johns Hopkins University in Baltimore, Dr. John Money uncovered more proof that body chemicals may cause people to fall madly in love. People who had part of the pituitary gland (which is located at the base of the brain) cut out due to disease were tested for signs of various feelings. They could not experience the "high" of romantic love, although they experienced a wide range of other feelings. The lack of romantic feelings in these subjects seems to result from the lack of certain chemicals being produced by the pituitary gland.

What triggers the release of such chemicals in the body? Is it the way our bodies answer a certain smile or a special kind of walk? No one knows. However, many love experts believe that the study of human behavior offers as much of a guideline to the mysterious territory of love as does the study of brain chemicals.

One such expert who questions the use of the word "love" itself is Dr. Dorothy Tennov of the University of Bridgeport in Connecticut. She points out that the word love has many different meanings. There's the parent-child kind of love, the childhood crush, and the husband-wife kind of love, just to name a few. Dr. Tennov hit on the word "limerence" to describe the feelings experienced in romantic love. Unlike other kinds of love, limerence is an all-or-nothing state. "Nobody is ever just a little bit limerent," Dr. Tennov says. And although a person may love many people, nobody is limerent about more than one person at one time.

Dr. Tennov is quick to point out that finding limerence is one of the most difficult voyages an explorer of the heart can make. A person has to chart a course to safe harbor past such dangers as loving someone too much, demanding too much, or giving too little. Making a mistake may lead to a great deal of pain. Yet limerence is one of the greatest and most exciting of all human adventures.

Other scientists have noted, however, that many people today are looking more for the warmth of a long-term relationship than the excitement of limerence. With the high rate of marriage breakups, the better route may be not to fall in love so hard or so fast.

But this does not mean that you should become timid in searching for your true love. As one expert put it, anyone looking for a love partner has to be as wise as he or she is bold.

So the next time the thermostat inside your heart goes haywire at the sight of the most perfect man or woman you've ever seen, remember to look down and see which bridge you've just crossed. Your heart may be pounding from fear instead of love. But, if love is what you want, by all means set sail on the most exciting journey of your life. Should the romance not work out, go out and buy yourself some chocolates. And how will you know when you're cured? When you find a new love.

Dan saves the whole town when he runs away.

The Runaway

by Sharon Hoover and Margie Hayes Richmond

Dan O'Connell played his banjo as his father and his older brother, Tom, gave the horses their evening feed.

"We don't need a concert," Tom snapped at his brother. "You never do anything practical."

Dan put down his banjo. "Pa, I'm leaving tomorrow," he said. "I'll get a job driving mules on the canal."

Tom rose. Although he was only sixteen—only a year older than Dan—he was a good deal taller. "That's a stupid idea."

"Well, you say I'm not much help here," Dan shot back.

Frank O'Connell spoke quietly to his sons. "The Grand Canal is going to bring money to the West, Dan. You don't need to seek it. And, Tom, don't be jealous of your brother's talent. Now to bed, both of you."

Dan climbed to the loft behind Tom. He lay down and listened to the chorus of baby frogs peeping in the night. When everyone was asleep, he tied his extra set of clothes in a roll, picked up his banjo, and slipped into the night.

Dan struck out for the canal. The ground was soft after too many days of rain. He could smell the canal before he could see it. He could hear its strange sucking sounds. He found himself wading in mud and seeping water. Then he saw the water flowing over the bank of the canal. The ground moved under him and his whole body was lifted by a wave. He scrambled back the way he'd come.

Dan knew the whole bank of the canal would soon give way. The water would flood the town, as well as the fields below. He climbed a tree and tied his roll of clothes and banjo to a branch. Then he came down and ran towards town.

Dan came to Bleeker's Inn first. He threw open the inn door. "Mr. Bleeker! Canal's broken!"

Mr. Bleeker wasted no words. "Big break?"

"The whole bank's giving way," Dan replied.

"We'll need the help of the hurry-up boat. It ought to be at Jake's Landing any minute. Take Dorral, my mare, and ride over there. I'll ring the church bells to wake the town."

Dan led the horse out of the barn and galloped down the road. A light appeared as Dan neared Jake's Landing. It came from the long, slender vessel that was the hurry-up boat.

"What's up?" the captain of the boat yelled in

response to Dan's waving arm.

"Break in the canal!" Dan answered.

"Where?"

"Above town," Dan said.

"Everybody out!" the captain bellowed. "You ride and wake the farmers, son. We'll need softwood to dam up the canal."

The boat moved off. Dan cut across the fields to the road, stopping long enough to wake the sleeping farmers. The nearest trees to the break would be on Cook's place. Dan galloped the horse there.

"Mr. Cook!"

"What in blazes is the matter, boy?" asked the sleepy-eyed man.

"Canal's broken. Water's running out. They'll need soft trees."

"Big break?" Mr. Cook asked.

"I think so."

"You'd better be certain," Mr. Cook warned, "or you'll be paying for the trees I cut."

Dan turned the horse. His own place was next. He hesitated. His pa might ask a lot of questions. Well, there was no avoiding it. Dan galloped the horse to the door.

"Pa! Pa!" Dan yelled. His pa's big frame filled the doorway.

"Canal's running out," Dan said. "Cook's going to cut trees to dam it up. You could take the team of horses to help him."

"Aye," his pa replied. "They'll be needing softwoods."

Dan turned the horse toward the canal, grateful that his pa hadn't asked anything—yet.

The hurry-up boat had arrived at the break. Dan led Dorral to the water to drink, then took her to the tree where he had tied his banjo. He wiped the mare down with his extra pants. "Good girl, Dorral."

Dan spotted the townspeople who had come to help. Some were building campfires. Others were slashing small trees for shoring up the edges of the break. The crew of the hurry-up boat was directing the logs into place to form a dam. The water was running out more rapidly, causing a fast, strong current in the canal.

"Poles!"

More logs were rolled into the water. Dan saw the end of one of the logs swing around in the fast-moving current. One man feeding the logs into the water lost his footing. Dan ran to the water and dived in. The man groaned and sank under a wave.

Dan grabbed the man and held him so the current wouldn't sweep him away. Another man jumped forward to help Dan lift the hurt man out of the water.

"Leg's broken," the man groaned.

Dan raced toward a group of townspeople, shouting, "Dr. Gray!" If the whole town was here, then the doctor would be too. "Dr. Gray!"

"Here," Dr. Gray answered. He was setting a broken arm.

"Man has a broken leg," Dan said.

"Bring a blanket here," the doctor said. "Then

we'll see to the other man."

Dan got a blanket and wrapped it around the man. Dr. Gray picked up his kit. Dan quickly led him to the man with the broken leg.

Dr. Gray felt the leg gently. "You rinse off the mud," he told Dan.

Dan did as he was bid, trying not to be clumsy.

"This is going to hurt now," the doctor told the man. "Lie across him, Dan, and hold him still."

The doctor went to work. As the man's body thrashed, Dan wished he had his brother's strength. After the doctor finished setting the man's leg, Dan covered the man with a blanket.

Just then a shout went up from the people working on the dam. The dam was holding. Dan looked around him. Everyone looked bent and dreary.

"What would you think of a cup of tea?" the doctor asked, a smile cracking his tired, drawn face.

"We could all use a little entertainment to cheer us, too," Dan replied.

"And how would you plan to entertain us?" the doctor said. "Have you a violin in your pocket so you could fiddle a melody?"

"No, but I've a banjo in a tree." Dan ran to the tree for his banjo. He started picking the strings quietly at first, then louder and louder.

The people raised their tired heads slowly, then some started to clap.

Dr. Gray put down his tea and grabbed his wife around the waist. Soon several couples were dancing in the middle of a large circle of clapping people. Dan's fingers picked faster and faster.

Finally, Dan threw up his hands. "That's enough for tonight, folks."

"You sure can pick a banjo," Dr. Gray said to Dan. "You've got musical style, rhythm, and a sense of melody."

Dan saw his brother and his father coming over and only sighed in reply.

His father immediately asked, "How did you come to find the break in the canal?"

"I was running away," Dan answered.

"I can't hold you if you really want to go," his father said. "But I sure wish you would stay."

"Yeah," Tom agreed. "The horses will miss your banjo playing at suppertime."

Dan looked at his brother sharply. "You mean you *like* my banjo playing?" he asked.

"I said the *horses* liked it," his brother growled.

Dan laughed. "C'mon," he said. "Let's go home."

THE GREAT BANK ROBBERY OF MENDHAM

by Arthur Myers

**The people in Mendham were disappointed—
even hurt—when the would-be bank robbers
stopped coming around.**

Mendham, New Jersey, probably had the longest
wait for a bank robbery in history. But then again,
the wait itself was splendid entertainment.

The two robbers were probably the least slick of
thieves. They first cased the bank in March of 1960.
They parked their car in front of the bank and
stared at it for a long time. Just about everybody in
town got a good look at them. Mendham has only
3,000 people, so when the two strangers parked their
vehicle in front of the bank and didn't even get out,
people noticed.

At the time, Police Chief Moore was shoveling snow a short distance down the street—in front of the police station, in fact. He noticed the strangers too. A clever man, the police chief began shoveling in their direction. As he came alongside their windshield, the visitors became nervous. They took off, leaving a cloud of exhaust smoke.

The next day three exciting things happened:

1. At 10:42 A.M., Chief Moore received a telephone tip that someone was planning to rob the Mendham bank.

2. At 1:12 P.M., the chief was standing on Main Street. A car pulled up in front of him. In it were the two visitors of the day before. They asked him for directions to a certain auto-body repair shop. The startled chief told them he had never heard of the place, and the strangers drove off.

3. At 1:44 P.M., the chief was strolling along Main Street. He happened to glance into the window of the Mendham Soda Shop, which

is a few doors from the bank. In the soda shop sat one of the men. The stranger sported a mustache and had a moon-shaped scar above his right eye.

From then on, everyone in town kept seeing the same car and the same two men, usually within a stone's throw of the bank.

The chief checked with police departments all over the state. In nearby Madison, he hit pay dirt. Apparently, the two robbers weren't the type to shrink from attention. A man in Madison had been boasting that he was going to knock off the bank in Mendham. "It would be easy," he said, "if you drew the coppers away from the center of town."

Another man in Madison had been carefully explaining to almost anyone who would listen how the robbery would be carried out. He and "one of the boys" were going to use a red 1950 Ford for the job. Then they would switch to an old Nash, parked on Ironia Road west of town, and away they would speed. The cops would never be able to follow them.

The upcoming robbery was a show that seemed to have everything—style, talent, a long line at the box office. Its two stars—the would-be robbers who were becoming so well-known in Mendham—were William Redic, an odd-jobs man, and Robert Grogan, a candy store owner. Redic was the one with the mustache and scar.

But suddenly the robbers stopped boasting, and they even stopped showing up in Mendham. The townspeople were disappointed, even hurt. What had gone wrong? Had the strangers found a better bank to rob?

Nine months later, a car with Redic at the wheel pulled up in front of the Mendham bank. This time, he actually went in. Redic approached Herbert Miller, the young man who managed the bank. Afterward, Miller reported that his visitor had been very nervous. That had made Miller nervous. Of course, Miller also knew who Redic was. Who in Mendham didn't?

Redic asked the banker about loans. They talked about this for a short time. Then Miller was called away to the phone. The call was from the butcher whose shop was across the street. He wanted to warn Miller that the bank robber had just gone into the bank.

"Yes, yes, I know," Miller hissed and hung up. Miller hurried back, just in time to see Redic get into his car and drive off. A lot of people in town were angry at the butcher. They believed his phone call had marred the robbers' rehearsal for the real event. They hoped the robbers hadn't been scared off for good.

But the robbers seemed to have found new courage, for Redic and Grogan began visiting Mendham every other day. Once, Redic pulled up to the bank's drive-in window.

"I want ten cents' worth of dimes," Redic said, his voice shaking. Then, his face reddening, he coughed and explained that he meant a *dollar's* worth of dimes. He got his dimes and, with half the people in town watching, drove to a nearby grocery store and bought a chocolate bar.

The robbers were now almost like old friends to the townspeople, but Chief Moore knew this was no time to relax. They might strike at any time, and he would look mighty silly if they pulled it off.

The chief planted his second-in-command—in fact, the only other person on the Mendham police force—Officer Cillo, next door to the bank. Officer Cillo's cover was painting a church. His gun hidden in a rain pipe, Cillo had most of the building painted, and the chief was desperately searching for another plan. Then what seemed like the Great Day arrived.

The day began with a mysterious phone call that a bomb had been planted in the school. "A likely cover for the robbery," the chief thought. The teachers and students left the building, and the police went into action. Chief Moore slipped over to the bank. Officer Cillo began painting closer to the rain pipe.

To everyone's disappointment, the robbers were spotted driving out of town.

But the next day—oh wonderful day of days—the robbers struck!

Herb Miller, the young banker, had stepped outside to drop his empty lunch wrappings in the garbage pail next to the bank. He saw the two robbers drive by. They went around the bank and drove by again. They drove by a third time. Then they parked down the street, got out, and started coming in Miller's direction.

"This might be it!" Miller thought. He hurried

into the bank to make ready. First he told one of his two tellers, Ann Neill, to head for the ladies' room. Then he turned to greet his visitors.

"I want to open an account," Redic said.

Miller handed him a form, and Redic went to a table to fill it out. Grogan and Miller stood talking about the weather.

Suddenly Grogan pulled out a gun. "Make no wrong moves and nobody will get hurt!" he cried.

Carefully making no wrong moves, Miller filled a cloth bag with $10,679 and extended his arm to hand the bag to Grogan. Just then the phone rang. When Miller answered it, Redic became so excited that he hit the banker. Then the two robbers pushed Miller and his other teller, Jerre Budd, into a supply room and tried to tie them up. But the ropes kept slipping, although the two bank workers tried to help. Finally the robbers gave up and ran for the door.

Outside waited Chief Moore, with troops: Officer Cillo had grabbed his gun from the rain pipe, and two other policemen had raced over from the next town. The robbers had been in the bank quite a while.

"Get 'em up!" ordered the chief.

They did, and that was the end of the Great Bank Robbery of Mendham.

Both the robbers went to prison.

There was a certain amount of sadness in Mendham, once the robbery was over. After all, for many months it had been the best entertainment in town.

Job Interview Tips

by Sylvia P. Bloch

Afraid of job interviews? Don't worry, help is here.

It's the middle of the night and you can't sleep. But you have to sleep. Tomorrow is the big day— it's your interview for that job that you really want. If you show up exhausted, how can you hope to do well? You wrestle with the pillow, but it's no use. Every muscle feels tight and you feel like you'll never relax, much less fall asleep.

Well, the good news is that you are not alone. Many people feel fear at the thought of looking for a new job, whether it's the first time or not. And the even better news is that there are ways you can prepare yourself so that you can go into that office and face the interviewer without it being a disaster.

Here are some tips for you to keep in mind when looking for a job and arranging for an interview. Remember, what may seem like a lot of preparation will actually go far in helping you face the challenge with a greater chance of success.

First of all when you are looking for a job, talk to everyone. You never know who may know of someone who is looking for a person to fill a job. Also, the more you speak with people in the field you are interested in, the more you will learn about that field. This will help you when it comes time for the interview, for the more you know about a job, the more you can share with the interviewer.

Read everything you can about the field you are interested in. Check the newspaper want ads. They are a good way to see what kind of jobs are out there as well as what the salaries are. Also think about going back to school. This doesn't have to mean years and years—it may be for only a class or two. Think of it as another way of getting information about a field that might interest you. Also, it is something that can be added to a resume to show that you have some education and background in that area.

When it comes time to prepare your resume—don't get scared. You don't have to use fancy paper or colors to grab someone's attention. The goal is to put down on paper a clear history of what you know and what you have done. Think about all the jobs you have had, including volunteer work and jobs you do without getting paid. For example, many women who re-enter the job market after being home with the children think, "I haven't done anything." But this is not true. You have to go back and think about all the skills you use in your everyday life.

Let's say you've done your job of talking to people, learning about your field of interest, and preparing your resume. Now let's say you hear about a job, either from talking to someone or reading the ads in the paper. Set up a time for an interview. Find out as much as you can about the company and make sure you know how to pronounce the interviewer's name correctly.

What happens next? It's time to rehearse! Ask a friend to role play with you. Have that person be the interviewer and run through a practice interview. The goal is not to know what you are going to say by heart, but rather to get experience in hearing different types of questions and answering them. You want to feel comfortable at the interview. So now is the time to think about how you are going to answer questions like these: "Why did you leave your last job? Why do you want this job? Where would you like to be in five years?" Ask the other person how you did. How did you sound? You don't want too many "Ahs" and "Ums" interrupting your answers. How did you look? You should sit up straight and look comfortable.

Once you are done rehearsing, make sure you give yourself enough time to go over what you are going to wear to the interview. Dress the way someone who already has the job would dress. Make sure your clothes are clean and ironed. It is best not to look too fancy or colorful.

Here it is—the day of the interview. You are well rested (no wrestling with pillows the night before), because you have followed the tips above. Give yourself plenty of time to get to the interview. You don't want to spend your time explaining away a flat tire or complaining about the bus that's always late.

When you get to the office, take a big breath. Then walk in, smile, and give the interviewer a firm handshake. Don't be afraid to make a bit of small talk before the interview gets underway. You want to show that you are friendly and interested in others—just don't overdo it.

When the interviewer asks you about your last

job and why you left it, it's best to tell the truth. But do it in a way that is fair. If you felt that your boss was always screaming and breathing down your neck, wanting to control everything you did, this is not the time or place to say so. Keep your feelings about the boss to yourself. Instead, say that you are the kind of person who works well alone and can take charge of a project. You should also ask questions about the company and the job in order to get a feel for what the working conditions might be like.

When it comes time to talk about what the job pays, wait for the interviewer to bring it up, or else

you might sound as if the money is the only thing that interests you. When you are asked about your salary at your last job, tell the truth here too. The interviewer can always check to see what you were actually making. If the interviewer asks you what salary you are hoping to make, you don't want to risk asking for too much or too little. A safe bet would be to ask the interviewer: "What do you usually pay people who do this job?" If it is still left up to you to come up with a number, think back to those want ads in the paper and what those salaries were.

Let's pretend that the interview went well and

the interviewer offers you the job. It sounds interesting, and you think this might be a nice place to work. But then the interviewer mentions the salary, and it's less money than you want or need. You don't have to say yes or no right away. You can try to ask for more money, but don't start in with, "But I need more money because I have to pay for college and my rent just went up." This will make you look as though the money is more important than the job. Instead, draw out the interviewer and see if there is a salary review in three or six months. Also ask what the benefits are. A job that covers doctor and hospital bills, for example, is worth a lot. Also, sometimes companies help pay for you to go to school to get more training for your job, which usually leads to a higher paycheck.

Sometimes an interview goes well, but you don't know right away if you have the job. Make sure to send a follow-up letter to thank the person for the interview and to show your interest in working for the company.

Remember, going on a job interview doesn't have to make you frantic. Just use these tips to help you relax and be a success.

**Johnny Myers confessed to the murder,
but Detective Stover is sure that Myers is lying.**

Murder One

by F. X. Duffy, Jr.

The ceremony was nearly over. Detective Captain Richard Stover sat in the back of the church. He listened to the minister speak: "Detective Sergeant Walter Evans, husband, father, member of this church, made the greatest sacrifice of all in giving his life in the line of duty."

Five days ago, Detective Walter Evans had been brought into General Hospital with a .38 bullet in his temple, another in his chest. Stover had been put on the case the same day by the chief of detectives. It didn't take Stover long to get the facts.

The night he was shot, Evans had gone alone to see Johnny Myers. Myers was an informer who had a long prison record. Apparently, Evans had gone to see Myers for information about the doings of Big Jim Karros, a drug pusher. Karros was somehow tied to a case Evans was working on.

A gun found near Myers' run-down hotel had broken the case wide open. It had Myers' fingerprints all over it. The lab matched bullets fired from the gun with the bullets taken from Evans' body. That, plus the fingerprints, made it very hard for Myers to deny killing the detective. In fact, Myers had confessed almost at once.

The D.A. had been pleased; the case was solved in near-record time. There was enough solid proof— even without Myers' confession—to go to trial and win. But it was also likely that Myers would go off to prison on a lesser charge than first-degree murder, thereby missing the gas chamber altogether.

Myers' lawyer had already entered a plea of guilty with explanation: Myers was high on drugs at the time of the shooting. Furthermore, the lawyer said, Myers had been frightened by Evans' rough manner of questioning and had shot the detective in self-defense.

Stover wasn't at all happy with this explanation, nor did he agree with the D.A. that the case was solved. Perhaps it was because one or two details of the case seemed too vague to the experienced detective. Or maybe it was because he and Walt Evans had worked together years ago, at Downtown

Homicide, and now Stover was at his funeral.

The choir began a sad hymn. Stover recalled how Evans used to laugh and say that good detectives solved tough cases with the help of a miracle or two. "I always thought it was hard work and a little luck, old friend," Stover thought. Then, as if to apologize, he bowed his head and said in a low voice, "Sorry your luck ran out, Walt."

Stover got up slowly and left the church. It was a dreary, overcast day. Stover, exhausted, headed for his unmarked vehicle. He'd spent the last two days and nights going over every detail of Myers' story. Something wasn't right, but Stover couldn't say exactly what. Maybe it was the fact that Myers never tried to deny shooting Evans. Having had a taste of prison life already, most ex-cons facing a possible murder-one rap would say anything to stay out of jail. But Myers had spilled his guts immediately after being collared.

Or maybe Stover was bothered by the fact that there were no witnesses to the shooting. Evans had been shot down near the docks around 9 P.M., a time when the whole area was usually crawling with drunks, drug pushers, and the like.

Myers' claim that Evans treated him roughly didn't make sense to Stover. Stover knew Evans' style. His ex-partner would try to scare an informer about as often as snow fell in July. But what bothered Stover most was the way Evans had died. "He was too good a cop for some punk to get the drop on him like that!" Stover thought angrily.

The detective's thoughts again turned to Myers' possible reasons for killing Evans. None of them made sense. "But would anyone confess to killing someone if he didn't do it?" Stover wondered. The idea seemed ridiculous, but for some reason Stover couldn't shake it.

Stover drove west toward the docks, thinking the case through one more time. On one hand, there was already a mass of details—the gun, the fingerprints, the confession itself—to support Myers' guilt. On the other hand, Stover had faith in his gut feeling that Myers was lying.

"If only there was a clue," Stover sighed.

Stover parked his car near the scene of the crime. A gust of wind from the harbor sent a shiver through him. He walked very slowly, his eyes covering every inch of ground before him. Both the crime lab and the homicide squad had already scoured the area.

Finally, he gave up. Miserable and totally exhausted, Stover started back toward his car only to trip on the corner of the sidewalk. Kicking it, he

hurt his toe on the sewer grating. He noticed that it was not securely in place. Stover slipped his fingers into the grating, then smiled. Using his handkerchief, he took out two small bottles stuck in the grating.

Minutes later, Stover pulled his vehicle into a parking space at headquarters and went straight to his office. He phoned the lab for an immediate pickup. He ordered fingerprint tests, as well as tests on the possible contents of the now empty bottles.

Three hours later, Stover questioned Myers in his prison cell. He looked the ex-con over carefully, noting that Myers' face was blank, his movements stiff.

"I have only one question, Myers," Stover began at last. "Seen a drug pusher named Big Jim Karros lately?" Stover saw fear leap into Myers' eyes.

"No," Myers answered quickly.

"You're lying," Stover said, pulling a sheet of paper out of his pocket. "This is a report from the lab on two small bottles I found near the scene of the crime. Your fingerprints are on both of them, and so are Karros'. Both bottles also showed traces of a very powerful knock-out drug." Myers blinked twice.

Stover moved in for the kill. "The lab also tested the shirt taken off of Evans' body. Seems a slight trace of the same drug was found there as well. Want to come clean, Myers?" Stover asked. "The presence of the drug proves Evans' death was planned. You're now facing the gas chamber, buddy."

The ex-con shot Stover a vicious look. Then Myers started talking. Very little of his story surprised Stover.

Karros had paid Myers—with drugs the ex-con badly needed—to meet Evans at the docks. At the last minute, Karros handed Myers the knock-out drug, threatening to kill Myers if he didn't throw it in the cop's face. Myers did as he was told. As Evans ducked to avoid the drug, Karros came out of the shadows, shooting.

Afterwards, Karros swung a deal with Myers. Either Myers confessed to the "accidental" shooting in exchange for a free supply of drugs in prison, or he could go to the gas chamber with Karros. "I'll tell the cops you were in on it with me," Karros had told Myers.

To Myers, a heavy drug user, a deal for free drugs in prison was better than the life he had been leading lately, much less the gas chamber. All Karros had to do after that was wipe his prints off the gun, give it to Myers, and disappear. With Evans dead, Karros figured he had all the time in the world to cover up his other murder—the case Evans had been working on.

Stover nodded when Myers finished. The drugs-in-prison deal didn't surprise him. It had, unfortunately, become a common practice in the overcrowded prison system. What amazed Stover was how he'd found the bottles in the first place.

"Completely against the odds," Stover thought. Was it a miracle or luck? Stover decided maybe it was a little of both, and thought again of his old friend.

**Alone in Mexico, ignored by her family,
Louisa Taylor drinks to block out her
sadness and pain.**

The Penny Children

Part 1

by Kay Jordan

The newspaper clipping burned slowly. To just
tear up the detailed account of her older daughter's
wedding ceremony hadn't seemed vicious enough.

Louisa felt completely abandoned as she watched
the flaming paper. Peggy had written about her
plans to marry and had half-heartedly apologized
for not including an invitation for her mother. Peggy
had said, "It's because I don't want you to feel
ridiculous."

That had been her children's excuse for keeping Louisa from all of their social events for two years. "We're concerned only about you," her children always said. But Louisa was intelligent enough to know that they were thinking only of themselves. No doubt, it was her own fault. She had set the example by never thinking of herself first when the children were growing up.

Louisa Taylor had spent her adult life in a small Texas town that bore her husband's family name. She had met her husband in college. He was a brilliant law student, and Louisa was filled with confidence that she would become a doctor. But after falling in love, that plan hadn't seemed practical. Jim would return home to run the family business, and her role would be to have children and help Jim by being involved in social functions. That, in fact, was how it had turned out.

Louisa never minded a life filled with cookies and football shirts. She thought of her children as a credit to her, and she was content to give her life entirely to them.

The problem began when Jim's father died. Jim had to take complete control of the family business. When Jim was away on business trips, Louisa was called on to make more and more sacrifices.

At first, Jim was gone just a weekend here and there. Louisa had to take over most of the family responsibilities, although she often felt taxed beyond her abilities as she tried to meet all the needs of four demanding children.

Then the Dallas trips began. Jim had to go there regularly. Soon Louisa noticed a change in Jim's usual expression. She said nothing. Whether it was business or another woman, Louisa didn't know. Whatever the reason, she and Jim were drifting apart. Being no philosopher, Louisa's theory on dealing with the unknown was to keep quiet and wait it out.

As the children grew older, Louisa decided to take an active part in Jim's business. She helped develop a better system of accounting and later took over the immense job of setting up a new laboratory for petroleum studies. She enjoyed the work, all the while refusing to take a salary, and traveled with Jim when possible. The faraway expression on Jim's face did not appear so frequently, and they were a happy couple again.

Louisa and Jim had more than just a few good years, although the children always made demands on their parents' time and money. The two older children went off to college, equipped with cars and enough money to ensure their getting into the right social set. The two younger children seemed secure, although they still expected Louisa to solve every problem for them.

Then Chris Lawson came into their lives. She was the new head of the petroleum laboratory. Chris had style, grace, and intelligence. Soon Louisa and Jim began entertaining Chris at dinner and at the country club. Although Chris was unmarried and had no children, she was always ready to take the younger Taylor children to play tennis or to jog. Louisa's children thought Chris was terrific.

One day, Louisa noticed an expression of longing on Jim's face as he looked at Chris. Louisa became suspicious, but she refused to discuss the problem with Jim. Louisa opposed admitting to, much less facing, a possible problem in their marriage. She simply froze her mind and feelings, refusing to give up an inch of the ground upon which she had built her life.

For the next year, Louisa hoped Jim would come to his senses. She refused to notice that Jim's absences from home began to multiply. Then the summer came, and all four children were home again.

At first, Louisa thought that her children felt for her. They seemed to sense what was going on and appeared to be shocked by their father's behavior. For weeks one or the other of them wouldn't speak to their father, and some nights the atmosphere at the dinner table was so grim that even Louisa couldn't bear it.

One day the girls came home from the country club in tears. They recounted every detail of what

they'd heard about their father's dinner date with Chris Lawson. Somehow the atmosphere in the house changed after that.

The children began to blame Louisa as much as they blamed their father. The girls each cried, "How can you stand it, Mother? How can you let him embarrass us like this? Everybody knows. Everybody! I can't hold up my head in town. I'm so miserable, I wish I could die." They pushed and pulled until nothing was left of the family structure.

Louisa didn't want to leave Jim, and Jim didn't know what he wanted. He didn't want to break up his marriage. On the other hand, he said he was in love with Chris and didn't see why he should have to give her up. Finally, Louisa made that decision for him. She and the younger children would leave. Louisa thought that was what the children wanted.

Louisa was horrified when the children said they didn't want to go with her. The two older ones returned to college; the younger children said that they couldn't possibly leave their friends! They couldn't spend their last years in a different school. Didn't she have any feelings at all? Didn't she realize what she was asking them to do?

Louisa wanted to take back her decision to leave Jim. But it would have taken a miracle to put the pieces of her marriage back together. She had taken a risk and lost. Once Louisa had made up her mind, Jim had made up his.

Jim and Chris were married six months later. Friends began to shrink away from her as the town's society got used to the idea of Jim and Chris being married. After all, Jim Taylor was the most important man in town, and some marriages were failures.

Louisa was angry that she had given up. She was angry that she was alone. She had to escape to a place where no one knew her. She decided to try Mexico. The family had gone there for a vacation once, and Louisa knew she could hide away there. She told friends that she planned to set up her own business in Mexico. But once settled in Mexico, Louisa pulled shut the curtains of her cottage and tried to drink away the hurt.

Her children wrote. They even came to visit, once. But Louisa couldn't take part in their lives without returning to the old world where they didn't want her to feel uneasy. They never gave Louisa a choice about witnessing the most important events in their lives—lives Louisa had sacrificed to make.

"Chris will stand in your place, Mom," they said unthinkingly, "so you don't need to feel bad for us. And that way you won't have to be embarrassed." Embarrassed? *They* were the ones who didn't want to be ill at ease. She had borne pain and embarrassment for years on their account. Still, life had been better then than the life of loneliness and regret she had now.

Louisa blew away the ashes of the burned clipping and poured herself another drink.

End of Part 1

Popo and Maria bring new meaning to Louisa's life.

The Penny Children

Part 2
by Kay Jordan

The noise of garbage cans falling over woke Louisa. She didn't know how long she had slept. Time for her was just a matter of counting off one more hour, one more miserable day. She had been sitting outside her cottage, drinking and watching a lizard walk across the adobe wall when she had dropped off to sleep.

Louisa stood up. She was sure that some hungry peasant was searching through her garbage for food. Although Louisa was a generous woman, she drew the line at stealing, even it if it was from her trash. To let any theft go unnoticed was an invitation to trouble.

Louisa walked through the gate of the wall surrounding the cottage. She expected to see a peasant running away. Instead, she found a tiny boy, smiling up at her. He was ragged and dirty and wore only one sandal. He kept smiling, so she smiled back. A look of pleasure spread across his face.

"Me help you," he said, not as a question but as a statement.

"You?" Louisa answered. "But you're only a small boy. Besides, I don't need help." She knew that she should go inside the house. Young Mexican boys could be very taxing, especially when they knew enough English to beg.

"Me bring sister to help," the boy insisted. "Maria," he called, and a very timid girl, smaller than he, stepped out from behind a can.

"You see," the boy said, smiling all the while. "We big help. You stay here." And the two ran off out of sight.

A few moments later, the children returned with flowers in their hands. Louisa knew the flowers grew wild in the fields, but she took them with a sense of pleasure. Her children had never given her flowers.

"These are splendid," Louisa told the two children. "Very nice."

"We go now. Come tomorrow," the boy said. The pair were off before Louisa could object.

The next day the two children returned as they had promised. The young boy's name was Popo. Louisa tried to speak with them in Spanish, but Popo and Maria insisted on speaking English.

"You teach me English. I pay you," Popo said. The thought of the tiny boy paying her was humorous to Louisa.

"No, you bring me flowers, so I pay you. How much?"

"We *give* flowers," Popo said. "Now your turn. You give words."

"All right," Louisa agreed. She spent an hour that day teaching them English. Popo or Maria would point to things and Louisa would name the objects in English. Then Popo asked if he and Maria could clean Louisa's yard "for a penny." Louisa grew suspicious. "Well, at least they're not outright beggars," she thought. The children worked hard, thanked her for the penny, and left.

The pattern repeated itself every day for a month. The children had a lesson, did a simple task for a penny, and then disappeared. Louisa called them her

"penny children."

Popo and Maria never begged and were always polite when she shared fruit with them. They were so unlike any children she had ever known. Once or twice Louisa tried to find out more about them. When they refused to answer her questions, she quit prying. She didn't want to lose them.

One day, Louisa invited Popo and Maria to go with her to an upcoming festival. Popo turned to Maria. "We discuss," he said and leaned his dark head over his sister's. They talked in Spanish in hushed tones.

"We come," Popo finally told Louisa. "We meet you by tourist place." Louisa agreed and began to look forward to something for the first time in years.

The day turned out to be terrific. The three laughed, ate tortillas, and drank colas while they watched the parade. Louisa was so pleased that she excused herself to go buy them souvenirs. Armed with ponchos and sandals, she was pushing her way

back through the crowd when she recognized a monk from the neighborhood mission. He was holding the children by the hand, pulling them along the street.

"Please, no," Louisa yelled and ran along after his trailing black robe. The monk stopped and turned as Louisa caught him by the arm. She explained that the children had accompanied her. The monk was not pleased.

"They manage to sneak out every day," he said.

"We worry not knowing where they are. I'm sorry they bothered you."

"They don't bother me," Louisa objected. "And they never ask for anything."

"Mission children don't beg," the monk answered. Then he looked at the children and said sternly, "Neither do they sneak away." Finally he said, "You may have them the rest of the day."

Popo and Maria were pleased with their gifts, but Louisa saw that they were afraid to accept them. Finally Louisa told them that she would ask the mission to let them keep the ponchos and sandals. Popo still seemed bothered. When Louisa asked why, his answer was vague.

Popo seemed very uneasy and would not meet Louisa's eye. Finally he said, "They know you, Señora Taylor. At the mission, they call you the Sad Señora."

The boy had meant the news in kindness, but Louisa felt a pang of pain. Of course everyone knew her, the American lady who drank. Who would want to trust her with young children? The three walked slowly to the mission. The children turned in at the gate and thanked Louisa for the festival. They didn't take the gifts.

Louisa walked home, feeling sorry for herself. The minute she got home, she poured herself a drink, then smashed the glass. That night Louisa didn't drink. The next day she went to the mission and asked to see its head. She was admitted to a small office where a Mexican native in a monk's robe looked up from his desk.

"I am the Sad Señora," Louisa   . "My real name is Louisa Taylor. Until I met Popo and Maria I hadn't felt anything for a long time. Although I'm still the Sad Señora, I would like your permission to let them come and visit me from time to time. I . . . I need them."

"Señora Taylor," the monk answered, "most people have problems of one sort or another. You need not confess."

"I'm not here to confess," Louisa interrupted. "I'm here to ask a favor. I want to do something for Popo and Maria. I'm exhausted from pain and failure, and I'm not ready to live for children again. But there must be something I can do for them."

Louisa stopped, unsure how to continue. The monk nodded kindly and waited.

"Today," Louisa went on, encouraged, "I'm going to visit the import companies in town and try to get a job. I know both English and Spanish, I have contacts in Texas, and I know about business. Once I have a job, maybe I could help care for Popo and Maria. Anyway, until that time I'd like you to let Popo and Maria keep these gifts." Louisa brought out the ponchos and sandals she had bought at the festival.

"Of course, Señora," the monk said. "Good luck, and I hope we will see you again."

"Thank you," Louisa answered and stood to go.

As Louisa made her way to the business district of town, she thought, "I never got more from a penny."

THE MOLDY STORY OF PENICILLIN

by Arthur Myers

Alexander Fleming discovered penicillin by accident. He didn't realize it was a wonder drug.

The great achievements in science have come about through hard work, great intelligence, a talent for rising above failure—and luck. And many a successful scientist has been quick to admit that the most important of all of these is luck.

This was certainly true of Alexander Fleming, discoverer of penicillin. When he was old, famous, and full of honors, Fleming often told his audiences: "I have been wonderfully lucky, you know." And it was true that luck was involved when Fleming gave an all-important second look at a dish he had thrown away.

In 1928 Fleming was studying a certain type of bacteria. He was growing the bacteria in small glass dishes in his laboratory in a London hospital. One day he came back from a vacation and threw away a number of dishes containing bacteria that had spoiled. Shortly after, one of his helpers came into the laboratory. Fleming wanted to instruct the assistant in the sort of dishes that should be thrown away. To demonstrate, Fleming showed the man the spoiled dishes he had tossed out. It was then that Fleming observed a mold growing along the edge of one of the dishes. It looked rather like the mold that is sometimes found on bread or cheese. Further, the bacteria next to the patch of mold seemed to be shrinking, drying up.

To a brilliant scientist like Fleming, there was immense importance in this discovery. Something made by the mold was able to destroy bacteria. Fleming decided to call it, whatever it was, *penicillin* (after the Latin name for a group of common molds).

Fleming grew some of the mold in a sort of soup. Then he strained this soup into what he called mold juice and, with a needle, introduced it into rabbits and mice to see if the juice was poisonous. It was not.

Fleming's friends remember his curious behavior. Fleming went around asking his friends whether they had any moldy old shoes lying around. If they did, he would take a little mold out of the damp, dark inside of the shoe, grow it in his special soup, then test it against bacteria. He wanted to see if various other molds had the same effect on bacteria as his penicillin. None of those he tried did.

In spite of his encouraging start, Fleming was not able to find out what the mold really was, how to keep it, or how to get the active penicillin—a by-product of the mold—out of the mold juice.

It was not until 1939, 11 years later, that a group of scientists addressed the problem. Gradually, they discovered the principle of getting the penicillin from the mold juice. But then the question remained, what exactly was it good for?

As a test, they gave healthy mice shots of deadly bacteria. Then they gave some of the mice shots of penicillin. Those who received penicillin got better. The others died. Penicillin, they demonstrated,

worked against bacterial diseases in mice. But a mouse is only a tiny fraction of the size of a human, a totally different animal. Next, the scientists were intent on discovering whether penicillin would work on human beings.

The scientists were terrified that they would lose the strain of mold from which they were getting penicillin. The time of these experiments was during World War II. England was under fierce bombing attacks from the German air force, which showed no respect for chemistry laboratories. To lose Fleming's original strain of bacteria would be a disaster. To guard against this, the scientists rubbed some of the mold on the insides of their pockets. Their theory was that if the laboratory were leveled by bombs, perhaps one of the team would escape death. If so, the strain of mold would be saved by being in that person's pocket.

The scientists asked British chemical firms to help by producing the mold in their laboratories, but the companies refused. The chemical firms were caught up in the wartime situation. They were busy making the chemicals needed for war, as well as medicines to save the soldiers' lives. They had no room or time to spare. The scientists were forced to go it alone and grow the mold in their own laboratories. This was quite a challenge. They used anything they could find—cookie tins, trays, pie dishes, even sixteen old-fashioned bedpans. The work went on for eight months before enough penicillin had been secured to treat one human being. Then they had to find a human subject.

In an Oxford hospital, a policeman was dying of a severe sickness. No medicine seemed of use. It appeared that he would perish. The doctors decided to try penicillin on this hopeless case.

"I remember very clearly," one of the team said later, "bicycling from the hospital to the laboratory with news of how the patient was doing. Our people danced with excitement at the chance of a great success in medicine."

The penicillin worked. For five days, the policeman's condition improved. Then the laboratory's hard-won supply of penicillin ran out. The man was not yet completely cured. Without penicillin, the bacteria multiplied in his body, and he died.

But the way had been pointed to a new miracle drug. With new faith in their efforts, the scientists stepped up their work, to the point of exhaustion. Soon they had produced enough penicillin to treat four sick children, and thereby saved the children's lives.

With a desperate war raging, it was important that enough penicillin be produced to treat the wounded. But Britain was under attack. The leaders of the team of scientists, Howard Florey and Ernst Chain of Oxford University, decided that the giant drug companies of the United States must be persuaded to mass-produce the new wonder drug. They were successful. Soon laboratories all over America were working on the drug.

Scientists also hunted for a better strain of

penicillin mold. All penicillin so far had come from the original patch that had grown on Fleming's dish back in 1928. Scientists based in Peoria, Illinois, had the job of finding a new mold. Air force people were asked to send molds from all over the world to the laboratory at Peoria. Many moldy things were received, but none were of help.

One laboratory worker in Peoria had the job of going to market every day and bringing back all the moldy fruit and vegetables she could find. As a result, her fellow workers fondly called her Moldy Mary. One day she brought back a moldy melon. On this melon was the mold they had searched all over the world for. Much of the penicillin used today came originally from that moldy piece of fruit. Luck had worked its magic again!

By 1943, penicillin was ready for use in battle. When American and British soldiers hit the beaches of Sicily and France, the drug saved thousands of lives. It seemed to truly be a miracle drug.

In 1945, after the war ended, Fleming, Florey, and Chain shared the Nobel Prize for Medicine.

Penicillin has saved the lives of hundreds of thousands of people since then. We have probably all been treated with it. Today it is only one of many such wonder drugs, and the search goes on for new and better ones.

Find the one correct answer.

Features of a
Short Story

1. _____ What is the setting of the story?
   a. The planet Sidec
   b. The planet Varck
   c. Earth
   d. In deep space

2. _____ Which of the following gives the
   most important event in the plot
   of the story?
   a. Sonia and Kato had been
   working on the alarm for three
   days.
   b. Kato let go of the tool in his left
   hand.
   c. The Throps attacked.
   d. Kato had blacked out.

Cause and
Effect

3. _____ The Earth machinery no longer
   worked because
   a. the Throps had destroyed it.
   b. the deep-space settlers had
   broken it.
   c. it had been left out in the
   vacuum of deep space for too
   long.
   d. robots hated to repair it.

Recognizing
Substitutions

4. _____ "Kato's grip slipped and he accidentally let go of the tool in his left
   hand. He muttered to himself as
   he saw it float upward, out of his
   reach." What does *it* in the second
   sentence stand for?
   a. Kato's hand
   b. The tool
   c. Kato
   d. The spaceship

5. _____ Which of your senses is the writer appealing to by saying: "Sonia would always remember the faces of the dead: screams of pain and terror sealed forever in icy masks"?
   a. Hearing and sight
   b. Smell and taste
   c. Touch and taste
   d. Taste and sight

6. _____ Which of your senses is the writer appealing to by saying: "She lay helpless in the small, shallow crater of her own making, listening to the sickening sound of a thousand Throp creatures squealing as they attacked"?
   a. Sight
   b. Hearing
   c. Touch
   d. Taste

7. _____ Kato thought Sonia was one of the best electronics experts around, whereas Sonia thought Kato was
   a. very brave.
   b. a bad worker.
   c. just a stupid robot.
   d. a funny little pet.

8. _____ What have you learned about Sonia?
   a. She doesn't like jokes.
   b. She is very brave too.
   c. She looks out only for herself.
   d. She is easily scared.

9. _____ What have you learned about Kato?
   a. He never jokes around.
   b. He's really a coward.
   c. He's a robot with a great spirit.
   d. He doesn't care if humans live or die.

Main Idea (10.)_____ What is the main idea of this story?
- a. Machinery should not be left out in a vacuum.
- b. Robots make up good jokes.
- c. Strange creatures live in deep space.
- d. Brave beings respect and care for each other.

Check your answers with the key.

EA-2 ▰▰▰▰▰▰▰▰ CANADA TO THE RESCUE

Find the one correct answer.

Features of a Short Story
1. _____ What is the setting of the story?
- a. Oregon
- b. Teheran
- c. A small town in Iran
- d. Canada

Sensory Images
2. _____ Which of your senses is the writer appealing to by saying: "As Lijek and King stood talking, a woman working at the embassy let out a squeal"?
- a. Sight   c. Touch
- b. Hearing   d. Taste

Sequence of Events
3. _____ Of the following four events, which one happened second?
- a. The Marines tried to radio for help.
- b. Iranian students started climbing over the walls of the U.S. Embassy.
- c. People inside the building talked about how cheap oil used to be.
- d. Lijek broke the printing plates.

141

4. _____ Lijek and the others decided to
leave the building because
   a. it was time for dinner and they
   were hungry.
   b. the area around the building
   looked clear.
   c. the revolutionary students told
   them all to leave.
   d. everyone in the building was
   just an ordinary citizen.

5. _____ Ambassador Taylor chose to put
the escape plan into action during
the election in Iran because
   a. this was when his friend at the
   Iranian Foreign Ministry would
   be free to help.
   b. the CIA had just sent special
   passports and false visas to
   him.
   c. the six diplomats were getting
   very bored and nervous inside
   the Canadian Embassy.
   d. there would be a lot of
   confusion throughout Iran,
   making it possible to get the
   six diplomats out of the
   country unnoticed.

6. _____ "The Americans who had escaped
didn't dare go to their own homes.
The Iranians would surely look
for them there." What does *them*
in the second sentence stand for?
   a. The revolutionary students
   b. The escaped Americans
   c. The U.S. Marines
   d. The Canadians

7. _____ Go back to the story to figure out which of the following gives the meaning of *grillwork*:
a. Guns used by Marines
b. A window that has a curtain in it
c. Iron bars protecting windows
d. Anything built so that it forms a screen

8. _____ How did Mrs. Taylor feel when someone telephoned her home and asked for two of the Americans in hiding?
a. Mrs. Taylor had a bad heart.
b. Mrs. Taylor felt afraid.
c. Mrs. Taylor was angry.
d. Mrs. Taylor enjoyed her conversation with the caller.

9. _____ Which of the following is the best summary of the story?
a. The U.S. Embassy in Iran was taken over by students.
b. Six American diplomats hid in Teheran after the U.S. Embassy was taken over by revolutionary students.
c. Ambassador Taylor visited the Iranian Foreign Ministry a lot during the time he hid the escaped Americans.
d. The six American diplomats who escaped capture by Iranians were rescued by the Canadian Ambassador in Teheran.

10. _____ What is the main idea of this story?
a. Ambassador Taylor was very brave to help American diplomats escape from Iran.
b. Iranian students had a right to

143

take over the U.S. Embassy in
Teheran.

c. The easiest time to escape from
any country is during an
election.

d. Iran is not safe for Americans.

Check your answers with the key.

Find the one correct answer.

Cause and
Effect

1. _____ At the beginning of the story, the
chicken yard was in chaos because

a. the Garrison children were all
laughing.

b. a dog was chasing the chickens.

c. Ralph had fed the chickens
something that made them
drunk.

d. Rachel dropped into the fertilizer pen.

Understanding
Character

2. _____ What have you learned about
Ralph?

a. He felt he was dumb and not
well liked.

b. He loved living on the farm and
being part of the church.

c. Jokes came naturally to him
and he wanted more out of
life than living on the farm.

d. His father liked him the most
when he played a joke on
everyone.

3. _____ Which of your senses is the writer
appealing to by saying: "He didn't
know why his parents couldn't
enjoy the clouds moving across
the horizon or the designs that
irrigation made in the soil"?
a. Sight
b. Hearing
c. Touch
d. Taste

4. _____ Which of your senses is the writer
appealing to by saying: "All Ralph
could see was a room full of
moving fans and water-soaked
handkerchiefs"?
a. Sight
b. Hearing
c. Touch
d. Taste

 _____ Why did Uncle Mott cast Ralph
only as the Devil in school plays?
a. Ralph was a very bad actor.
b. Ralph was very naughty.
c. Ralph was too tall to play
another part.
d. Ralph looked mean, just like
the Devil.

 _____ What does the writer mean by
saying that the stuff in the bottle
Jim left behind would put hair on
Ralph's chest?
a. The stuff was some kind of
medicine for growing hair.
b. The stuff should have been
rubbed on the chickens, not
drunk.
c. The stuff is a kind of glue.
d. The stuff was a strong drink
that could get anyone very
drunk.

145

7. _____ Go back to the story to figure out which of the following gives the meaning of *onstage*:
a. Part of a farmyard
b. A playground near a school
c. A place where actors do plays
d. The living room of a house

8. _____ What does the writer mean by: "Uncle Mott pulled at his hair until it looked like the top of a pineapple"?
a. The top leaves of a pineapple are used for wigs.
b. Uncle Mott wore the top of a pineapple as a hat.
c. Uncle Mott pulled at his hair until it stood on end.
d. Uncle Mott had no hair on his head.

9. _____ What do you think Ralph will do next?
a. Ralph will soon learn to be a good boy.
b. Ralph will write a book about the Devil.
c. Ralph will go on having trouble obeying rules as he grows up.
d. Ralph will be hurt badly in a farm accident.

10. _____ What is the main idea of this story?
a. Ralph is very different from the rest of his family.
b. Kids who joke around too much should be kicked out of school.
c. Something interesting is always happening on a farm.
d. Playing jokes will never get you into trouble.

Check your answers with the key.

Find the one correct answer.

Features of a
Short Story

1. _____ Who are the main characters?
   a. Ralph and Mrs. Brown
   b. Rachel and Ma Garrison
   c. Ralph and Mr. Brown
   d. Ma and Pa Garrison

2. _____ What is the tone of this story?
   a. Happy and filled with joy
   b. Scary but funny
   c. Filled with hope
   d. A bit sad and angry

3. _____ Which of the following gives the most important event in the plot of the story?
   a. Ralph loses Sarah Logan because of his drinking and card playing.
   b. Mr. Brown offers Ralph a job.
   c. Pa Garrison won't let Ralph accept the prize money for the painting of Rachel.
   d. Ralph, his father, and Mrs. Brown travel to the state art contest in Oklahoma City.

Recognizing
Feelings

4. _____ When Ralph sighed and took out his art pad, how was he feeling?
   a. Sad because he no longer had the warmth of close relationships
   b. Tired of always drawing
   c. Hungry because it was almost dinnertime
   d. Angry at all the rules that surrounded his everyday life

Write _T_ if the sentence is true; write _F_ if it is false.

Real or
Make-Believe

5. _____ Ralph was really on the prairie when Mrs. Brown asked him about his drawing.

Find the one correct answer.

Making
Inferences

 _____ Why did Mrs. Brown give Ralph private art lessons?
  a. She thought Ralph had a lot of skill.
  b. She'd always wished to have a child of her own.
  c. She wanted to come between Ralph and his parents.
  d. She needed more money.

 _____ Why did Ralph's parents support his art?
  a. They wanted him to win a lot of money in contests.
  b. They thought having an interest would keep their son from drinking and playing cards so much.
  c. They wanted their son to become famous.
  d. It was the only useful thing Ralph did.

 _____ When Ralph was boarding the train, why did Pa Garrison grab Ralph and kiss him?
  a. To have Ralph send him money
  b. To surprise Ralph and get in the last word
  c. To show Ralph he loved him
  d. To make Ralph sorry about leaving

Predicting
Outcomes

9. _____ What do you think will happen
next?
a. Ralph will drown at sea.
b. Ralph will never talk to his
father again.
c. Ralph will change his mind and
go to a church school.
d. Ralph will one day settle his
differences with his father.

Main Idea

⑩._____ What is the main idea of this
story?
a. Never enter an art contest.
b. Ralph and his parents have
trouble understanding each
other.
c. Most good artists were bad as
kids.
d. Being a parent is a difficult job.

Check your answers with the key.

EA-5 ▇▇▇▇▇▇▇▇▇▇▇▇▇▇▇▇ **RALPH, PART 3**

Find the one correct answer.

Features of a
Short Story

1. _____ What is the setting of the story?
a. A ship and a train
b. A navy base in the United
States
c. Washington, D.C.
d. A navy base and the Savages'
farm

2. _____ Who are the main characters?
a. Myrtle and Jake
b. Congressman Savage and Pa
Garrison
c. Ralph and Mrs. Savage
d. The ship's captain and officers

3. _____ What is the tone of this story?
   a. Happy and funny
   b. Sad but with a happy ending
   c. Scary throughout
   d. Very angry

4. _____ Which of the following gives the most important event in the plot of the story?
   a. Bill Savage breaks his arm and leg.
   b. Congressman Savage laughs at Ralph's stories.
   c. Ralph decides to see his dad before it's too late.
   d. Ralph paints a picture of the captain.

Write _T_ if the sentence is true; write _F_ if it is false.

Real or
Make-Believe

5. _____ Ralph only dreamed that his parents had died.

Find the one correct answer.

Recognizing
Feelings

6. _____ How did Bill Savage feel when he heard his father had died?
   a. Very sad
   b. Angry
   c. Happy
   d. Scared

7. _____ At the Savage farm, when Ralph remembered the rooster from his dream, how did he feel?
   a. Full of hate for his parents
   b. Very scared that his parents might die
   c. Very angry at Mrs. Savage for giving him the east room
   d. Very happy that Bill had asked him to come along

8. _____ When Mrs. Savage said good-bye to Ralph, how was she feeling?
a. Angry at Ralph for leaving
b. Scared for her son
c. Sad about her husband's death
d. Worried about Ralph

Summarizing

9. _____ Which of the following is the best summary of the story?
a. Bill and Ralph get in trouble with the navy.
b. Bill's father dies and Ralph realizes he loves his parents while at the Savages' farm.
c. Ralph paints a picture of the captain and decides to go back to the farm.
d. Mrs. Savage gives Ralph the east room, but Ralph is scared of the rooster.

Main Idea

10. _____ What is the main idea of this story?
a. Congressmen love to hear good jokes.
b. Ralph finally learns how to accept his parents and live his own life.
c. Good artists drink, play cards, and hate their parents.
d. Parents never hear from their children once their children grow up.

Check your answers with the key.

Write *T* if the sentence is true; write *F* if it is false.

Fact or
Opinion

1. _____ The statement that the Tower of London is "now one of the leading attractions in Britain for vacationers" is an opinion.

2. _____ The statement that "the Tower has a fabulous collection of ghosts" is a fact.

3. _____ The statement that "even today an atmosphere of dread hangs over the Tower" is an opinion.

Fact or
Theory

4. _____ The statement that "human spirits remain where they have experienced strong feelings in life" is only a theory.

Find the one correct answer.

Important
Details

5. _____ Who ordered the building of the Tower of London?
a. King Henry VIII
b. William, a Norman duke
c. Gruffyd of Wales
d. George, Duke of Clarence

Cause and
Effect

6. _____ "Traitors' Gate" got its name because
a. people were shot there during World War II.
b. many state prisoners believed to be traitors were brought through it to the Tower.
c. anyone walking through it would become a traitor.
d. a famous traitor built it and named it after himself.

7. _____ When Lord Lovat was going to
lose his head, how did he feel?
a. He felt honored that he'd been
picked.
b. He felt very sorry about all the
awful things he'd said about the
king.
c. He felt overjoyed to see some of
his enemies die.
d. He felt very calm because he'd
paid the axman a big tip.

8. _____ How did Margaret, Countess of
Salisbury, feel about losing her
head on the block?
a. Kind and forgiving
b. Very angry because she was not
guilty
c. Too proud to complain
d. Too scared to say a single word

Using Context
Clues to Find
Word Meanings

9. _____ Go back to the story to figure out
which of the following gives the
meaning of *bayonet*:
a. An ax with a long handle
b. A sword used in the 1800s
c. A long knife at the end of a rifle
d. A one-shot handgun

Main Idea

(10.) _____ What is the main idea of this
story?
a. England has had a lot of high-
ranking criminals.
b. Lots of people visit the Tower
of London today.
c. The Tower of London has a
bloody history.
d. Being beheaded is a painless
way to die.

Check your answers with the key.

Find the one correct answer.

Features of
a Short Story

1. _____ What is the setting of this story?
   a. A desert in Mexico
   b. The main office of Petron, a big oil company
   c. An oil rig in the Gulf of Mexico
   d. Larry's seaside vacation house

2. _____ Who are the main characters?
   a. Major Jenkins and Larry
   b. Lucy and the soldiers
   c. Big Jim Santos and Lucy
   d. Larry and Lucy

3. _____ Which of the following gives the most important event in the plot of the story?
   a. Lucy radios from Rig 22.
   b. Larry flies soldiers to Rig 23.
   c. Larry finds out Lucy is a colonel.
   d. Divers try to locate the oil leak.

Sensory
Images

4. _____ Which of your senses is the writer appealing to by saying: "We took off in a swirl of fog, which was soon replaced by howling winds"?
   a. Sight and taste
   b. Sight and hearing
   c. Touch and hearing
   d. Taste and touch

Word
Pictures
5. _____ What does the writer mean by: "I suddenly remembered that Lucy didn't take kindly to being treated like a breakable china doll"?

a. Lucy's bones broke easily, like china.
b. Lucy had a painted face.
c. Lucy was small and looked weak.
d. Lucy had always hated dolls.

Making
Comparisons
6. _____ Larry was a helicopter pilot, whereas his sister Lucy was

a. a housewife.
b. the owner of Petron Oil Company.
c. a helicopter pilot too.
d. a government agent.

Cause and
Effect
7. _____ International terrorists were bombing oil rigs because

a. they were bored and out of work.
b. they wanted to cripple Western nations.
c. they liked to watch oil-slick fires.
d. companies like Petron underpaid the workers.

Recognizing
Substitutions
8. _____ "A huge black oil slick stretched out over the ocean. It was hundreds of yards long, and getting bigger by the minute." What does *It* in the second sentence stand for?

a. The ocean
b. Yards
c. The oil slick
d. Minute

155

9. _____ When Lucy sighed and sank into the chair, how was she feeling?

   a. Sad that the terrorists were caught
   b. Relieved and overcome by exhaustion
   c. Lonely for her mother
   d. Angry that her brother now knew she was a government agent

Main Idea

(10.)_____ What is the main idea of this story?

   a. Terrorists are bad people.
   b. The army carries out many secret missions.
   c. Women are as able as men to carry out important jobs.
   d. "Big Oil" is an easy target for terrorists.

Check your answers with the key.

EA-8 ▪▪▪▪▪▪▪ THE SHY COUNTRY DOCTOR

Write *T* if the sentence is true; write *F* if it is false.

Fact or
Opinion

1. _____ The statement that Robert Koch "proved that anthrax was caused by one type of bacteria" is an opinion.

2. _____ The statement that Koch's "findings, along with those of Louis Pasteur and others, paved the way for such medical advances as vaccinations and wonder drugs like penicillin" is a fact.

Finding
Proof

3. _____ Look back to the story to find proof. "Koch did not believe in the germ theory of diseases."

Find the one correct answer.

Making
Comparisons

4. _____ The world's leading scientists had expensive equipment and helped each other with problems, whereas Robert Koch found the cause of anthrax
a. with the help of his teacher.
b. by borrowing expensive equipment.
c. without expensive equipment or help from anyone.
d. by getting lots of advice from other scientists.

Cause and
Effect

5. _____ No cure for diphtheria, cholera, or tuberculosis was possible back then, partly because
a. people were too frightened of catching these diseases to study them.
b. the causes of these diseases were unknown.
c. everyone who got these diseases died painful deaths.
d. scientists didn't care about finding cures for these diseases.

Making
Inferences

6. _____ Why did Robert Koch decide to study anthrax while a district medical officer?
a. His wife asked him to.
b. He wanted to teach his neighboring farmers a lesson.
c. Koch owned a lot of farm animals and was worried about them.
d. Koch wanted to prove the theory that living carriers spread diseases.

Using Context
Clues to Find
Word Meanings

7. _____ Go back to the story to figure out
which of the following gives the
meaning of *microscope*:
a. A kind of bacteria
b. Equipment used for seeing very
tiny life forms such as germs
c. Equipment used for looking at
stars
d. A special place where anthrax-
sick animals were kept

Sensory
Images

8. _____ Which of your senses is the writer
appealing to by saying: "Koch
saw cells shaped like rods
spread across the pure food inside his special airtight slides"?
a. Sight
b. Hearing
c. Touch
d. Taste

Recognizing
Substitutions

9. _____ "After finishing sketches of the
rod-shaped bacteria and its spores,
Koch used a needle to shoot the
spores into white mice. They all
perished from anthrax." What
does *They* in the second sentence
stand for?
a. The spores
b. Rod-shaped bacteria
c. White mice
d. The sketches

Main Idea

10. _____ What is the main idea of this
story?
a. Anthrax is a horrible disease.
b. Science was easier to study 100
years ago.
c. Robert Koch was a great
scientist.
d. Shy country doctors make
good scientists.

Check your answers with the key.

EA-9 ■■■ A WOMAN'S PLACE IS IN THE HOME?

Write *T* if the sentence is true; write *F* if it is false.

Fact or Opinion

1. _____ The statement "A woman's place is in the home" is a fact.

2. _____ The statement "There are almost 54 million women working in the United States today" is an opinion.

Find the one correct answer.

Using Context
Clues to Find
Word
Meanings

3. _____ Go back to the story to figure out which of the following gives the meaning of *mining*:
   a. Planting trees
   b. Cutting down trees
   c. Building factories
   d. Digging for coal

Cause and
Effect

4. _____ Many Appalachian mothers are entering the job market at a younger age than other mother's because
   a. their husbands want them to.
   b. they have their babies at a younger age.
   c. their children don't mind.
   d. they are in a hurry to get back to work.

Making
Inferences

5. _____ Why don't husbands want their wives to go to work?
   a. They cannot get used to the idea of their wives working outside the home.
   b. They fear their wives will no longer need them.
   c. They think their wives will not be able to keep up the household.
   d. They are angry when their wives find a job and they cannot find one.

6. _____ Which group of people are a growing part of the job market?
   a. Women who have never been married
   b. Men with steady jobs
   c. Married women with children
   d. Men who are married

7. _____ What have you learned about Emmy Owens?
   a. She's a person who gives up when things get difficult.
   b. She feels she doesn't need her husband anymore.
   c. She believes in staying home just like her mother and grand-mother did.
   d. She takes charge of her life and works to make things better.

8. _____ How do many of the Appalachian men feel when their wives get jobs?
   a. They feel good about themselves.
   b. They are happy for their wives.
   c. They feel angry and confused.
   d. They are happy that they don't have to work.

9. _____ "But Sarah, along with many others like her, found a way to feel better about herself. She heard of a free program, and it helped her see that there were things she could do." What does *it* in the second sentence stand for?
   a. Sarah
   b. Others
   c. A free program
   d. Things

Main Idea ⑩ _____ What is the main idea of this story?
a. Women should have children and stay home.
b. Women who work never stay married.
c. All men want their wives to take care of them.
d. Men and women have to change with the times.

Check your answers with the key.

EA-10■■■■■■■■GHOSTS ON THE HIGH SEAS

Write *T* if the sentence is true; write *F* if it is false.

Fact or Opinion
1. _____ The statement that "spirits haunt many a vessel" is an opinion.

Finding Proof
2. _____ Look back to the story to find proof. "*The Great Eastern* was the largest ship ever to be built up until its time."

Find the one correct answer.

Making Inferences
3. _____ Why does the writer choose to believe in ghosts?
a. He himself has seen them.
b. He knows sailors tell only the truth.
c. He wants to tell the readers a few ghost stories.
d. He himself is a ghost.

Understanding Character
4. _____ What have you learned about Captain Fokke?
a. He cared about his crew.
b. He had great courage.
c. He was very humble.
d. He was a horrible man.

5. _____ What does the writer mean by:
"More than once he had come
within a hair's breadth of losing
his captain's license"?
a. He had trouble breathing.
b. His license almost blew away in
the wind.
c. He came very close to losing his
license.
d. His crew kept trying to steal his
license.

6. _____ Which of your senses is the writer
appealing to by saying: "On her
unending voyage, the craft often
changes color, shape, and size"?
a. Sight
b. Hearing
c. Touch
d. Taste

7. _____ Captain Fokke's angel was rough
on sailors, whereas the ghost
Joshua Slocum saw was
a. even rougher.
b. a great help to him.
c. the same spirit.
d. a vicious goblin.

8. _____ Go back to the story to figure out
which of the following gives the
meaning of *white elephant*:
a. A big ship
b. Anything that is too expensive
and troublesome to keep
c. Any ghost on a ship
d. A gray-white paint used for
ships

9. _____ Go back to the story to figure out
which of the following gives the
meaning of *scrap dealer*:
a. A person who builds ships

b. A person who gets rid of ghosts
c. A person who buys and sells junk
d. A person who loves white elephants

Main Idea

(10.)_____ What is the main idea of this story?
a. Ships are scary.
b. Ghosts are kind only to good people.
c. Storms and big ships are dangerous.
d. Sailors tell many ghost stories.

Check your answers with the key.

EA-11 ▬▬▬▬▬▬▬▬▬▬▬▬▬▬▬▬ STRESS

Write _T_ if the sentence is true; write _F_ if it is false.

Real or
Make-Believe

1. _____ The hiss came from a poisonous snake.

Fact or
Theory

2. _____ The statement that "everyone reacts to certain kinds of situations—like emergencies, for example—with some degree of stress" is only a theory.

3. _____ The statement that such things as noise and overcrowding produce stress is a fact.

Fact or
Opinion

4. _____ The statement that "stress can trigger serious sickness in a victim" is a medical fact.

5. _____ The statement that "few people can avoid stress outright" is an opinion.

163

Find the one correct answer.

Important Details

6. _____ How many tranquilizers, anti-depressants, or sleeping pills do Americans take each year?
   a. One billion
   b. One hundred thousand
   c. Five billion
   d. Two billion

Using Context Clues to Find Word Meanings

7. _____ Go back to the story to find which of the following gives the meaning of *alcoholism*:
   a. Headaches from stress
   b. A state of alarm
   c. The need to drink
   d. A need to sleep

Cause and Effect

8. _____ People who have absorbed all the stress they can take get drowsy because
   a. they are scared to death that they'll see something horrible.
   b. their bodies have burned up many more calories than normal.
   c. they are always taking drugs to relax.
   d. they feel stress at the end of a long day.

Recognizing Substitutions

9. _____ "Many people turn to drugs or alcohol when this daily build-up of stress becomes too much to live with. They do so because severe stress itself becomes threatening to a person." What does *They* in the second sentence stand for?
   a. Drugs and alcohol
   b. Stress
   c. Daily build-ups
   d. Many people

164

(10.)_____ What is the main idea of this story?

a. Stress is no longer a health problem today.

b. Drugs and alcohol are the best ways to relax.

c. Severe stress can harm you unless you find healthy ways to relax.

d. Overcrowding isn't so difficult to deal with these days.

Check your answers with the key.

EA-12 ■■■■■■■■■■■■■■■■■■■■■OUTLINES

Find the one correct answer.

Features of a
Short Story

1. _____ What is the setting of the story?

a. Jim Frisk's house

b. A college

c. New York City

d. The office of a construction company

2. _____ Who are the main characters?

a. Connie and Jim Frisk

b. Adam and Lisa

c. Adam and Connie

d. Connie and Lisa

3. _____ What is the tone of this story?

a. Scary   c. Sad

b. Funny   d. Hopeful

4. _____ Which of the following gives the most important event in the plot of the story?

a. Adam argues with his dad.

b. Adam meets Connie.

c. Adam sends his dad a telegram.

d. Connie fights with her parents.

5. _____ Jim Frisk wanted Adam to finish college, whereas Adam wanted to
   a. get married immediately.
   b. study acting in New York.
   c. finish his college education too.
   d. join his father's company.

6. _____ How was Adam feeling when he shouted to his dad: "It's my life!"
   a. Happy about his life
   b. Joyful about his acting
   c. Angry at his father
   d. Sad about his future

7. _____ How did Connie feel when Adam realized she was blind?
   a. Sorry for herself
   b. Angry at the world
   c. Scared that Adam would no longer like her
   d. Amused by Adam's surprise

Write _T_ if the sentence is true; write _F_ if it is false.

8. _____ Adam was really in a swamp full of moving shapes and outlines.

Find the one correct answer.

9. _____ What have you learned about Jim Frisk?
   a. He was trying to live his life through his son.
   b. He blamed his wife and son for everything.
   c. He didn't care about his son's education.
   d. He was afraid of growing old.

Main Idea (10.)_____ What is the main idea of this story?
a. Fathers should decide what their sons should do.
b. Everyone has to decide on his or her own life outline.
c. A father is always right.
d. Going to college is the most important thing in life.

Check your answers with the key.

EA-13 ■■■■■■■■■ THE SECRETS OF LOVE

Find the one correct answer.

Making Comparisons
1. _____ One bridge over the Capilano River was well-built and modern, whereas the other was
a. well-built but higher.
b. a crude, narrow footpath.
c. wider and even more modern.
d. just like the other bridge.

Cause and Effect
2. _____ Millions of people are angered by research into love because
a. it costs too much.
b. they don't want scientific explanations for love.
c. no one cares about love anymore.
d. research in other fields, like energy resources, is more important.

Important Details
3. _____ People experience falling in love as
a. only a feeling of wondrous joy.
b. aching regret.
c. both wonderful and dangerous.
d. being no different than eating chocolates.

167

Write _T_ if the sentence is true; write _F_ if it is false.

Fact or
Theory

4. _____ The following statement is a fact: "Love, like any other feeling, is only the result of a chemical or two floating around an overworked body."

Fact or
Opinion

5. _____ The statement that "more young people today than ever before are attracted by the abandon and distress of romantic love" is an opinion.

Finding
Proof

6. _____ Look back to the story to find proof. "Most people want someone like themselves to love."

Find the one correct answer.

Drawing
Conclusions

7. _____ What led the writer to conclude that the chemical found in chocolate might one day cure lovesickness?
a. People always give chocolates as gifts to their loved ones.
b. Heartbroken people found relief by eating chocolates.
c. People who eat chocolates never fall in love.
d. Chocolate cures some kinds of coughs.

Using Context
Clues to Find
Word Meanings

8. _____ Go back to the story to figure out which of the following gives the meaning of "_love junkies_":
a. People who must always be in love
b. People who love to take drugs
c. People who believe love is a lot of garbage
d. People who collect old things from junkyards

168

9. _____ Go back to the story to figure out which of the following gives the meaning of *limerence*:
   a. A parent-child kind of love
   b. A childhood crush
   c. A love for adventure
   d. A romantic kind of love

Main Idea

(10.) _____ What is the main idea of this story?
   a. Only poets should write about love.
   b. Scientists are now studying love to find out its secrets.
   c. Love junkies walk across unsafe bridges.
   d. Love research makes people angry.

Check your answers with the key.

EA-14 ▬▬▬▬▬▬▬▬▬ THE RUNAWAY

Find the one correct answer.

Features of a
Short Story

1. _____ What is the setting of the story?
   a. A swamp
   b. The Grand Canal
   c. A treetop
   d. Bleeker's Inn

2. _____ Who is the main character?
   a. Dorral
   b. The captain of the boat
   c. Dr. Gray
   d. Dan O'Connell

3. _____ What is the tone of this story?
   a. Sad   c. Angry
   b. Exciting   d. Funny

4. _____ Which of the following is the most important event in the plot of the story?
a. Tom feeds the horses.
b. The hurry-up boat comes to Jake's Landing.
c. Dan finds a break in the canal.
d. Dr. Gray asks Dan to play the banjo.

Sensory Images

5. _____ Which of your senses is the writer appealing to by saying: "He lay down and listened to the chorus of baby frogs peeping in the night"?
a. Sight   c. Touch
b. Hearing   d. Taste

Making Inferences

6. _____ Why did Tom snap at his brother about playing his banjo instead of doing something practical?
a. Tom was jealous of Dan's musical talent.
b. Tom hated his younger brother.
c. Tom thought music upset the horses.
d. Tom wanted to listen to the chorus of frogs.

Cause and Effect

7. _____ At the end of the story, Dan went home because
a. he left his banjo in a tree.
b. Dr. Gray danced to his music.
c. he realized his brother and father loved him.
d. he was caught by his father before he could get away.

Making Comparisons

8. _____ Tom was best at doing practical things, whereas Dan
a. wanted to become a doctor.
b. liked to play the banjo.
c. rode horses for fun.
d. drove mule teams on the canal.

Predicting
Outcomes

9. _____ What do you think Dan will
become when he grows up?
a. The captain of a hurry-up boat
b. A doctor
c. A banjo player
d. A grocery store owner

Main Idea

10. _____ What is the main idea of this
story?
a. Canals are dangerous.
b. Farmers need sons who do
practical things.
c. The Grand Canal brought lots
of money to the West.
d. Brothers can be very different
and still love each other.

Check your answers with the key.

EA-15 ████████ THE GREAT BANK ROBBERY
OF MENDHAM

Find the one correct answer.

Features of
a Short Story

1. _____ What is the setting of the story?
a. Mendham, New Jersey
b. Ironia Road
c. Inside a police station
d. In a Ford car

2. _____ Who are the main characters?
a. Jerre Budd, Ann Neill, and
Herbert Miller
b. The 3,000 people in the town
c. William Redic, Officer Cillo,
and the butcher
d. William Redic, Robert Grogan,
and Police Chief Moore

3. _____ What is the tone of this story?
   a. Very sad and hopeless
   b. Too scary for words
   c. Somewhat funny and exciting
   d. Deadly serious

4. _____ Which of the following gives the most important event in the plot of the story?
   a. Officer Cillo paints a church.
   b. Chief Moore sees Redic in the soda shop.
   c. The butcher telephones Miller, the banker.
   d. Redic and Grogan finally rob the bank.

Recognizing Feelings

5. _____ How did the townspeople feel when the robbers stopped showing up in town?
   a. Frightened and unsure
   b. Relieved and happy
   c. Terribly disappointed
   d. Proud of their police officers

Word Pictures

6. _____ What does the writer mean by saying: "The upcoming robbery was a show that seemed to have everything—style, talent, a long line at the box office"?
   a. A movie of a bank robbery was going to be made.
   b. Everyone in town thought it would be the biggest event in years.
   c. People always look forward to a bank robbery.
   d. The bank was selling tickets to the robbery.

7. _____ Go back to the story to figure out which of the following gives the meaning of *marred*:
a. Enjoyed c. Ruined
b. Robbed d. Frightened

8. _____ "There was a certain amount of sadness in Mendham, once the robbery was over. After all, for many months it had been the best entertainment in town." What does *it* in the second sentence stand for?
a. Mendham
b. The bank robbery
c. Months
d. Entertainment

9. _____ Which of the following is the best summary of the story?
a. Two robbers spent months planning a bank robbery but were caught.
b. Mendham is a small town with a newly painted church.
c. Captain Miller shovels snow, Officer Cillo paints a church, and the butcher calls the bank at the wrong time.
d. Police Chief Moore meets two would-be bank robbers.

10. _____ What is the main idea of this story?
a. Robbing a bank in a small town takes planning.
b. Waiting for the bank robbery was entertaining for everyone in Mendham.
c. Police officers in small towns shovel snow and paint churches.
d. Robbers should never go to small towns.

Check your answers with the key.

173

Write *T* if the sentence is true; write *F* if it is false.

Finding
Proof

1. _____ Look back to the story to find proof. "Many people are happy at the thought of looking for a new job."

Fact or
Opinion

2. _____ The statement "It is best not to look too fancy or colorful" is an opinion.

3. _____ The statement that "sometimes companies help pay for you to go to school to get more training for your job" is a fact.

Find the one correct answer.

Sensory
Images

4. _____ Which of your senses is the writer appealing to by saying: "Every muscle feels tight and you feel like you'll never relax"?
   a. Sight
   b. Hearing
   c. Touch
   d. Taste

Making Inferences

5. _____ Why does the writer say that you should know how to pronounce the interviewer's name correctly?
   a. You will impress the interviewer.
   b. You might make a bad impression if you say the person's name wrong.
   c. The writer wants to make you nervous.
   d. The writer is making a joke.

Using Context Clues to Find Word Meanings

6. _____ Go back to the story to figure out which of the following gives the meaning of *resume*.
   a. A list of your education and past jobs
   b. A letter on fancy paper
   c. A history book
   d. A list of people looking for jobs

Cause and Effect

7. _____ The writer says that you should rehearse an interview because
   a. you might get a part in a play.
   b. it's fun to do with a friend.
   c. your friend might give you a job.
   d. it will help you feel more comfortable at the interview.

Recognizing Substitutions

8. _____ "Check the newspaper want ads. They are a good way to see what kind of jobs are out there as well as what the salaries are." What does *They* in the second sentence stand for?
   a. Want ads
   b. A good way
   c. Jobs
   d. Salaries

9. _____ Of the following four events, which one happens last?
   a. You write a follow-up letter to thank the interviewer.
   b. You prepare your resume.
   c. You pick out what to wear for the interview.
   d. You talk to everyone you can.

Main Idea (10.) _____ What is the main idea of this story?
   a. Everyone is afraid of job interviews.
   b. Always be on time.
   c. There are ways to prepare for a job interview.
   d. A resume should be short.

Check your answers with the key.

EA-17███████████████████ **MURDER ONE**

Find the one correct answer.

Features of a
Short Story

1. _____ Who is the main character?
   a. The chief of detectives
   b. Big Jim Karros
   c. Johnny Myers
   d. Detective Captain Richard Stover.

2. _____ Which of the following is the most important event in the plot of the story?
   a. Evans is brought into General Hospital.

b. Myers' fingerprints are found on the gun.

c. Stover finds two small bottles.

d. Myers is arrested.

Understanding Character

3. _____ What have you learned about Johnny Myers?

a. He cares a great deal about other people.

b. He's a loser who will do anything for drugs.

c. He showed great courage when Stover questioned him.

d. He is a crazy man who loves to kill.

Word Pictures

4. _____ What does the writer mean by saying: "But Myers had spilled his guts immediately after being collared"?

a. Myers got sick from the drugs he took.

b. Myers wore shirts with tight-fitting collars.

c. Myers confessed right after he was arrested.

d. Myers knocked over his glass when a police officer grabbed him by the collar.

Cause and Effect

5. _____ Stover didn't believe Myers' story about Walt Evans' death because

a. Big Jim Karros had confessed to his part in the murder.

b. Evans had left Stover a letter listing all the facts.

c. Stover believed in miracles.

d. Evans was too smart and experienced to get killed in the way described by Myers.

6. _____ Go back to the story to figure out
which of the following gives the
meaning of *ex-con*:
a. A person who eats a lot
b. A person who has spent time in
prison
c. A drug user
d. Anyone who lies

7. _____ Whose fingerprints were on the
bottles Stover found?
a. Evans' and Myers'
b. The D.A.'s and Stover's
c. Karros' and Myers'
d. His own and Myers'

8. _____ What led Stover to conclude that
Myers was lying?
a. A mass of evidence
b. Myers' confession
c. Stover's faith in his own gut
feeling
d. The way Myers' lawyer talked

9. _____ Why did Karros kill Evans?
a. To keep Evans from shooting
him first
b. To frighten Johnny Myers into
paying him money
c. To get even with Evans for
having once sent him to jail
d. To keep Evans from proving
that he had murdered someone

10. _____ What is the main idea of this
story?
a. Solving a crime sometimes
takes a little luck.
b. Good detectives are often shot.
c. Drugs are bad for people.
d. Ex-cons should never confess
to a crime.

Check your answers with the key.

Find the one correct answer.

Features of
a Short Story

1. _____ What is the setting for most of the story?
   a. A small town in Texas
   b. A college
   c. Dallas
   d. A newspaper office

2. _____ Who is the main character?
   a. Chris Lawson   c. Peggy
   b. Louisa Taylor   d. Jim Taylor

3. _____ What is the tone of this story?
   a. Exciting and vicious
   b. Funny and joking
   c. Angry and sad
   d. Happy but scary

4. _____ Which of the following gives the most important event in the plot of the story?
   a. Louisa wanted to become a doctor.
   b. The newspaper clipping burned slowly.
   c. Jim Taylor was a brilliant law student.
   d. Louisa left the family for Mexico.

Using Context
Clues to Find
Word Meanings

5. _____ Go back to the story to figure out which of the following gives the meaning of *philosopher*:
   a. Someone who works in a laboratory
   b. Someone who lives in Mexico
   c. Someone who thinks about the meaning of life
   d. Someone who regrets having been born

Drawing
Conclusions

6. _____ What led Louisa to conclude that her children thought only of themselves?
a. Peggy wrote about her plans to marry.
b. They always had an excuse for not inviting her to their social events.
c. They never sent her money.
d. She always felt ridiculous around them.

Word
Pictures

7. _____ What does the writer mean by saying: "She simply froze her mind and feelings, refusing to give up an inch of the ground upon which she had built her life"?
a. Drinking made Louisa a cold, unfeeling person.
b. Louisa wanted the house and the land.
c. Louisa put her head in the refrigerator whenever she was troubled.
d. Louisa couldn't admit that her marriage was in trouble.

Recognizing
Feelings

8. _____ How did Louisa feel about herself after she moved to Mexico?
a. Happy to be free
b. Very hurt and bitter about her selfish husband and children
c. Jealous of all rich people
d. Tender toward her children

Predicting
Outcomes

9. _____ What do you think will happen next?
a. Louisa will make up with Jim.
b. The children will beg Louisa to come back.
c. Louisa will meet new people who will treat her better.
d. Louisa and Chris Lawson will become best friends.

180

(10.)_____ What is the main idea of this story?
a. Mexico is a nice place to visit.
b. Raising a family is easy when you're rich.
c. People can be unthinking and unfeeling, even in families.
d. Parents should sacrifice everything for their children.

Check your answers with the key.

EA-19 ▬▬▬▬ THE PENNY CHILDREN, PART 2

Find the one correct answer.

Sensory Images

1. _____ Which of your senses is the writer appealing to by saying: "The noise of garbage cans falling over woke Louisa"?
a. Sight
b. Hearing
c. Touch
d. Taste

Recognizing Feelings

2. _____ When the boy gave Louisa flowers, how did she feel?
a. Jealous of her own children
b. Afraid he was a beggar
c. Pleased, since her children never gave her flowers
d. Tired and badly in need of a drink

Understanding Character

3. _____ What have you learned about Popo and Maria?
a. They were as selfish as Louisa's children in Texas.
b. They were poor and kind to others.
c. They were frightened and sad children.
d. They cared only about money.

4. _____ Go back to the story to figure out
which of the following gives the
meaning of *monk*:
a. Someone who loves going to
festivals
b. Someone who hates children
c. Someone who works in a
church mission
d. Someone who speaks both
Spanish and English

5. _____ The children returned every day
for a month and
a. spoke only Spanish.
b. each time did a simple task for a
penny.
c. begged for food.
d. answered all of Louisa's questions
about themselves.

6. _____ What does the writer mean by
saying: "Armed with ponchos and
sandals, she was pushing her way
back through the crowd..."?
a. Ponchos and sandals can be
used as weapons.
b. Louisa hid a gun under her
poncho.
c. Louisa was carrying ponchos
and sandals as she walked
through the crowd.
d. Louisa had strange hands and
arms.

7. _____ The monk was pulling the children
along the street because
a. they had sneaked out of the
mission, and he was taking
them back.
b. he was angry because the
children had begged.

c. he was trying to save them from Louisa's anger.

d. the festival was over and it was time to go home.

Making Inferences

 8. _____ Why did everyone call Louisa the "Sad Señora"?

a. She had sad-looking clothes.

b. She told jokes poorly.

c. She was very sad and troubled.

d. All people from Texas feel sad in Mexico.

Features of a Short Story

9. _____ Which of the following gives the most important event in the plot of the story?

a. A garbage can falls over and Louisa wakes up.

b. All three go to a festival and have a wonderful time until the monk appears.

c. Popo and Maria turn down Louisa's gifts and return to the mission.

d. Louisa stops drinking and looks for a job so she can help care for Popo and Maria.

Main Idea

 10. _____ What is the main idea of this story?

a. Mexico is an interesting place in which to live.

b. A penny can't buy much these days.

c. The best way to get over being hurt is to help others.

d. Monks are understanding people.

Check your answers with the key.

Find the one correct answer.

Important
Details

1. _____ Which has been the most important reason for many successful scientists' great achievements?
   a. Working hard
   b. Great intelligence
   c. A talent for rising above failure
   d. All of the above, plus luck

Making
Inferences

2. _____ Why did Fleming say, "I have been wonderfully lucky, you know"?
   a. He was very humble.
   b. All his other experiments had been failures.
   c. Luck was involved in Fleming's looking again at the all-important dish.
   d. Other scientists were the ones who did most of the work, not Fleming.

Sequence
of Events

3. _____ Of the following four events, which one happened third?
   a. Fleming threw away some dishes with bacteria that had spoiled.
   b. Fleming came back from vacation.
   c. Fleming showed a helper which dishes to throw out.
   d. Fleming observed a mold growing in one of the thrown-out dishes.

4. _____ "Fleming observed a mold growing along the edge of one of the
dishes. It looked rather like the
mold that is sometimes found on
bread or cheese." What does *It* in
the second sentence stand for?
   a. Mold
   b. Bread
   c. Cheese
   d. Edge

5. _____ The mold Fleming found was
growing, whereas the deadly
bacteria right next to it was
   a. growing even more.
   b. shrinking, drying up.
   c. changing color.
   d. starting to attack Fleming's
      mold.

6. _____ Penicillin wasn't really tested until
1939, 11 years after Fleming
discovered it, because
   a. no other scientist knew about
      Fleming's mold.
   b. scientists didn't believe Fleming's
      discovery.
   c. a way to get the penicillin out of
      Fleming's mold juice had to be
      discovered first.
   d. scientists already knew exactly
      what the mold was good for.

185

Write _T_ if the sentence is true; write _F_ if it is false.

Finding
Proof

7. _____ Look back to the story to find proof. "The scientists never asked anyone to help them produce mold."

8. _____ Look back to the story to find proof. "The policeman in an Oxford hospital died when the supply of penicillin ran out."

9. _____ Look back to the story to find proof. "Penicillin has saved the lives of hundreds of thousands of people since 1939."

Find the one correct answer.

Main Idea

10. _____ What is the main idea of this story?
   a. The Nobel Prize for Medicine is hard to get.
   b. A true miracle drug was found with the help of a little luck.
   c. Molds are very poor disease fighters.
   d. Scientists the world over search for mold.

Check your answers with the key.

ANSWER KEY

EA-1	EA-2	EA-3	EA-4	EA-5
1. b	1. b	1. c	1. a	1. d
2. c	2. b	2. c	2. d	2. c
3. c	3. a	3. a	3. c	3. b
4. b	4. b	4. a	4. a	4. c
5. a	5. d	5. b	5. F	5. T
6. b	6. b	6. d	6. a	6. a
7. a	7. d	7. c	7. b	7. b
8. b	8. b	8. c	8. c	8. c
9. c	9. d	9. c	9. d	9. b
10. d	10. a	10. a	10. b	10. b

EA-6	EA-7	EA-8	EA-9	EA-10
1. T	1. c	1. F	1. F	1. T
2. F	2. d	2. T	2. F	2. T
3. T	3. c	3. F	3. d	3. c
4. T	4. b	4. c	4. b	4. d
5. b	5. c	5. b	5. a	5. c
6. b	6. d	6. d	6. c	6. a
7. c	7. b	7. b	7. d	7. b
8. b	8. c	8. a	8. c	8. b
9. c	9. b	9. c	9. c	9. c
10. c	10. c	10. c	10. d	10. d

EA-11	EA-12	EA-13	EA-14	EA-15
1. F	1. b	1. b	1. b	1. a
2. F	2. c	2. b	2. d	2. d
3. T	3. d	3. c	3. b	3. c
4. T	4. b	4. F	4. c	4. d
5. F	5. b	5. F	5. b	5. c
6. c	6. c	6. T	6. a	6. b
7. c	7. d	7. b	7. c	7. c
8. b	8. F	8. a	8. b	8. b
9. d	9. a	9. d	9. c	9. a
10. c	10. b	10. b	10. d	10. b

EA-16	EA-17	EA-18	EA-19	EA-20
1. F	1. d	1. a	1. b	1. d
2. T	2. c	2. b	2. c	2. c
3. T	3. b	3. c	3. b	3. c
4. c	4. c	4. d	4. c	4. a
5. b	5. d	5. c	5. b	5. b
6. a	6. b	6. b	6. c	6. c
7. d	7. c	7. d	7. a	7. F
8. a	8. c	8. b	8. c	8. T
9. a	9. d	9. c	9. d	9. T
10. c	10. a	10. c	10. c	10. b